A Beginners Guide to Software Deployment

Dennis B. Waldon

DEDICATION

To Ricarda, my wife, for her encouragement and enthusiasm
To Mr. K, for being such an inspiration
To Paul, for his honesty when reviewing the text
To Gert, for teaching me how to unite real IT with real People

CONTENTS

ACKNOWLEDGMENTS

Acknowledgements to my friends at The NetWorker, who stuck with me through thick and thin when it came to working, brainstorming, and sometimes even downright guessing. It was great!

Thanks to many at Novell, you guys make great products that are fun to work with. Keep it up!

Thanks to all our loyal customers and friends who got us busy with software deployment, easy packaging and not!

Introducing...

Hi! My name is Dennis B. Waldon. As of writing this book I am 33 years old and live in southern Germany. I have a German / American background and work as an IT Consultant in the larger region of southern Germany for the last 12 years.

For whom is this book?

This book is for IT administrators, consultants and all those interested in getting a broad view of what it means to deploy software in a small and large IT environment. It should serve to give you a broad look at what technologies are available, and what it could mean for you.

There are dozens of books covering detailed aspects of software deployment; they are mostly focused on a certain technique or software product, but getting "the big picture" is sometimes hard to find in one compact volume.

Why I wrote these pages.

I started out with software deployment a few years ago. We had a company that was switching their operating system environment, and since we had some experience with "packaging" and distributing software with other customers, we were asked to equip their new environment with automated software installations.

Browsing through various bookstores and searching online, there were plenty of books and sites that went into detail into the various aspects of the bells and whistles of software deployment; but they never focused on a beginner or someone who wanted to get an overall view.

Sales representatives will offer you software suites and appliances galore, but most of the time customers don't know how to tell what they need, what they really want, and if that piece of software is really the right tool.

Some companies will do well with a software suite with a nice price tag; others do just as well with simple yet powerful tools.

The goal of this book.

The goal of this book is to help you:

- ... lean back and see software deployment as a whole, and then drill down to what suits *you* and *your* work best.

- get an overall impression of software deployment techniques

- look "under the hood" of some of the mechanisms that involve software deployment

- get a feel for what is expected of you should you decide to continue on.

Part 1: The Introduction

The first three chapters are dedicated to the absolute basics of software distribution.

- What are the main elements of software deployment?
- What are the steps involved in the creation of an application?
- What exactly is a program installation?

Picture 1 - Picture author / source: http://www.photocase.de/cydonna

Chapter 1: The Basics

The 4 Steps of Software Deployment

Software deployment is the "art" or summary of basically 4 steps[1]:

- Installing
- Configuring
- Maintaining and
- Managing

your applications and operating systems (clients and servers): regardless of a few machines or for an entire enterprise.

All of these steps are defined by you, your budget, your aims and environment.

This book is designed to help you lean back and see software deployment as a whole, and then drill down to what suits you and your work best. **There is no one-size-fits-all**: please read this book, take notes and after a while you will get the picture of what further steps you want to take.

Back to the roots
Historically, one of the main jobs of a Help Desk or Administrator is to run from machine to machine, user to user and to install applications.

Downside? Time and energy. You have plenty of other tasks to take care of.

Upside? Keeps you on your toes, you keep in touch with workmates, and you aren't locked in that lonely office all the time.

---

[1] http://de.wikipedia.org/wiki/Softwareverteilung

Seriously:

This method costs time and energy; time and energy that is more often than not spent again and again for the same purpose. With time, your environment is a jungle of

- Software

- Software versions

- Patches of different eras

- Configurations that are most of the time defined on the fly.

And this is what causes the cycle of *more* work: your environment is unpredictable, causes problems, and keeps you busy putting out little fires all the time and never really smoothing out your environment.

A strategy, however it may be, and we will have a look at these later on with you, will help you keep your environment in more or less **one unified state**. This dramatically reduces time and effort, as all software units are basically installed the same and have the same configuration.

This saves time in upkeep and maintenance:

- All machines "behave" the same in any given scenario

- Testing and changing your environment is made easier, as all clients all have the same prerequisites and baselines

- you save time dramatically

- you, your users can depend on your environment more, and react more efficiently.

The Roles being played

Professionally deploying software is seeing the different **roles** or even **viewpoints** involved.

Oftentimes, one single person fulfills all of these roles; in larger departments, knowledge and workflow is distributed among personnel.

Role 1. The Analyzer.

- What is the right software for a certain need?

- What are the costs involved?

- How easily is it installed "out of the box?"

- What is involved in upkeep?

- Has this software proved itself "in the wild"? Reviews, ratings, recommendations give great insight into your cost and benefit analysis.

The person using the software often does not see the necessity of answering these questions. They basically read the description or get a recommendation; they then want you to buy the box and install it for them.

Done. Finished. So what's the big deal, right?

Well, not quite right. Most manufacturers put all their resources into developing their application, but hardly into distributing it at the client's site. Once the box leaves the counter or the verification email is sent, customers are on their own. Analyzers do not take help resources and support for granted.

Role 2. The Product Supporter.

Those distributing software most probably do not know the workings of them. If you are an IT guy or gal, those financial analysis programs or bookkeeping software or the measurement software in the labs are not necessarily your one and only fields of expertise. A question to ponder: Who is most fit to fill the gap between user (with no IT knowledge) and IT department (who has no expertise with the software or the drive behind them)?

Most programs or software suites are well documented by the manufacturer, and sometimes even better by 3rd parties. Important fact to always find out: is there a direct helpline to the manufacturer or not? Will it cost? If yes, are you or your customer willing to pay for it?

Customers and their administrators often run into trouble, and if the software manufacturer is a one-man show and hardly reachable, or the support given is shady, or seemingly way too expensive, it may be worthwhile to shop around for an alternative.

Role 3. Product Maintainer.

Due to the ever changing work environment, updates and configuration changes are standard. No programs (or users for that matter) stay "put" and work happily ever after.

Here are some questions the Maintainer is confronted with every day:

- How often do you **want** to implement updates? (is there a need to always stay up to date? Think about the following saying: *"Never touch a running system!"*)

- How often do you **have** to roll out updates? (Users may need updated functionality, security measures, etc.)

- How will you test these before you roll them out?

- How can quality control be assured? Both of the program and the data involved?

Role 4. Product Manager.

Somehow, all of this has to be kept in one, nice and neat, manageable box. And in that box (we are speaking metaphorically here), we want to keep:

- Documentation (of the software itself & how it is utilized in your environment)

- Licensing Records (One time license fees, maintenance fees, serial numbers, etc.)

- Software Accounting (how to keep **what** you have installed **where**)

This kind of documentation, however you do it (be it a simple Excel file or a software management suite) is essential.

Why? you will be able to:

- easily determine what a change to your environment actually costs in terms of **time and money.**

- benchmark! How often would you like to explain to users and management what software deployment actually involves, again in terms of time and money invested? Pulling out numbers and examples will give your argument, whatever it may be, a solid foundation.

- upkeep a unified, structured environment, helping all in the long run. The user has a stable environment, the administrator has control, and management knows what is going on IT-wise in figures and numbers.

These roles are best defined in a simple documentation. Yes, defined. This may seem awkward at first, but it will help you and others see what is involved and stick to it!

With the help of documentation, dependencies and conclusions can easily be derived, new challenges are met with confidence and it is something that helps us all in the long run.

Chapter 2: A typical piece of software

If you have a look at a typical "piece" of software, be it a simple application for making screenshots or a complex office suite, most of them "tick" pretty much alike. You have your typical:

Operating Systems

Many programs are written specifically for different operating systems and hardware (="Platforms".) Not all programs run on 32 or 64 bit platforms for example; certain operating systems are too old or even too *new* to support a certain application.

Even the detailed versions of these software- and hardware platforms play an important role, as programs are very much dependent on the environment of the system they are on (which coincide with software dependencies, explained in the next part). We will only cover software deployment for 32bit and 64bit Microsoft Windows systems.

Software dependencies

These are "environments" that a program needs in order to run. Not all programs are capable of running completely on their own. Software programs like Java and .Net are so-called "frameworks" or "runtimes", or offer "libraries" that programmers can depend on in order for his or her program to run, saving development time (basic operations don't need to be reinvented over and over again) and creating uniformity.

Software dependencies help you and the software manufacturer to have a program that runs smoothly almost anywhere.

The Program Components

These are the actual files of a program. These include code written by the manufacturer, help files, support files and configuration files. In a classical environment, programs install themselves with the help of an "Installer" program into the programs directory of a system; the location of the installation may or not be important or flexible, depending on the application.

Program Settings

The settings of a program are not necessarily kept together with the actual software files; this was done a lot earlier (.ini files, .cfg files stored these settings in the file structure), but has developed in different ways.

Windows Registry settings (a kind of database that the Windows operating system keeps) are more and more the place where programs keep stock of their parameters, which are often shared with other programs.

Chapter 3: From start to finish

To understand how a program installs itself, let's have a brief look at how a program is created in the first place.

From scratch.

A programmer has a tough life: he has to be able to speak different languages and be able to read between the lines of all of them. Literally.

Programs of different types need different programming languages, and not all fulfill the same need in the same way. Then he has to be able to interpret the human mind: It is his or her job to "apply" the idea of a program, write it, and publish it.

And there you have your "application" of this idea.

The writing.

The programmer develops either specifically for a certain platform (Windows Version X) or he or she tries to write a program that is "cross-platform": a program that will run in various scenarios.

Java is such an example: A programmer writes the program, and it is essentially launchable from a Windows, Mac or Linux client. As mentioned before, depending on where the program is to be used and how, he or she can choose from a large library of languages: C, C Sharp, Visual Basic, these are run-of-the-mill languages for Windows native programs.

If the program designers are thinking web applications (applications that run from your browser), HTML, PHP, CSS and the likes in connection with databases are one of many choices. Some programs even mix elements.

The packaging

With the core files of the program, further files like help files, configuration files, add-on programs that are needed are added. And to distribute it (the installation part on the client), he or she will either have to program something that will:

- check the environment on which it is installing itself (perform an operating system check, dependency checks, enough space on the drive, etc.)

- Do the actual installation (copying files, configuring the client and its settings)

- Check if all operations of installing were completed successfully.

Now, the work is done, and all should be well. What options a programmer has to package and distribute the programs, and how you as the software caretaker manage this on a larger scale of clients is what we will discuss in the next chapter.

Part 2: you are what you Deploy

In the next 5 chapters, we want to have a closer look at what makes an installer tick, and then introduce a few market-leading installers that you most probably will come across.

Picture 2 - Picture author / source: http://www.photocase.de/cydonna

Chapter 4: Distribute Part 1 - Know your Tools!

Now we are getting close to the "lets get our hands dirty" part. But first, an introduction.

Before we get into the details of various installers, we should take a look at a list of elements that pretty much all installers have in common.

Components of a program installer:

- **Wizards**. Not the magical kind, but an interface that guides the User through the installation. A typical wizard will ask you for information about you or your company, where the program is to be installed, license information and other options and settings. These wizards can also be automated, and we will discuss this in 3 points further down the list.

- **Logging**. This is what will help you a lot. Never underestimate the value of logging. This tells you what went well during the installation, what went awry, when and where. Good logging means that the installer program records what steps and errors it encountered. Some installers require that you activate the logging and the level of logging (from basic to detailed).

- **Environment Checks**. An installer, when given the signal to start, will check things like if there is enough space on the client it is installing, if certain program dependencies are fulfilled, if you are installing on the right platform, etc. It either then gives a warning and halts, or it offers to install the missing components for you.

- **Silent Installation Modes**. Deployment of software shouldn't be a point-and-click-through-every-single-step for every software setup. It is possible to give the program all of the information it needs from the start without you or any user having to interact (=silent). This is where silent installation is a necessity. "Silent" has different modes (we want to concentrate on two):

Mode 1: Completely silent.

The program isn't visible at all while installing. Depending on the size and resources-hunger the program has, the user may or may not notice that an installation is running. Downside is that the you or the user won't be able to tell when the installation is done. you will either have to have set an action to happen when the installer is finished installing or check a log file.

Mode 2: Basic Silent Mode.

The program is partially visible during install (it may show a progress bar, but not much more). Upside is that the user sees that something is happening and doesn't have to guess when the program is installed. It also saves a call to the IT Hotline to ask why his or her computer may be slowing down during the installation, as they can see the progress of the installer.

Now we want to have a look at some of the major installers and options that are in use.

Chapter 5: The Windows Installer

The Windows Installer is more or less the standard procedure for software installations and rollouts. Applying patches, customizing installations and uninstallation is made fairly simple. Troubleshooting with the help of return codes and logging, repairing "broken" installations is all made simple with the Windows Installer.

The Windows Installer is usually already installed in your windows client and server environment; you could consider it as a framework that revolves around software installation management on a local scale.

By typing "*msiexec.exe /?*" from the command prompt you can already see options of the Windows Installer.

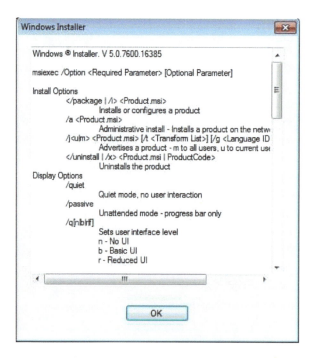

Picture 3 - Windows Installer options

The MSI file.

you will recognize a Windows Installer package when it has the file ending: *.msi.*

This MSI is basically a container: it holds the information required to install, modify and uninstall a program; it includes or points to the files need for installation (cabinet files or other files).

The MSI basically offers the software packager a way to organize the installation into components and features (explained a bit farther along this chapter).

Following is a list of features of a typical MSI file.

The Product Code

The product code is a special identifier for a product. It has the format **{xxxxxxxx-nnnn-yyyy-kkkk-123456789123}** or has a more "readable" name in the Windows Registry. (Letters and numbers are just placeholders in this case).

Each of these product codes are one of a kind; product versions and their translations all have a different code, even if they are the same program version. you will find a list of the programs installed on your computer if you have a look at the Windows Registry in

[HKEY_LOCAL_MACHINE\SOFTWARE\Microsoft\Windows\CurrentVersion\Uninstall\.

We will see an example of the Windows Registry where uninstallation information is saved on the next page.

Dennis B. Waldon

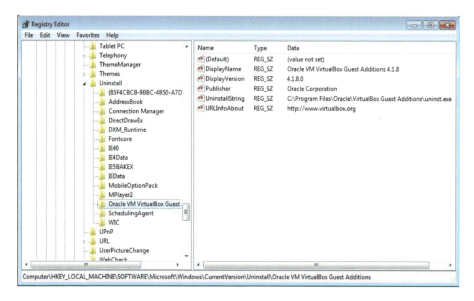

And this is what you see correspondingly in the Control Panel in *"Programs and Features"*:

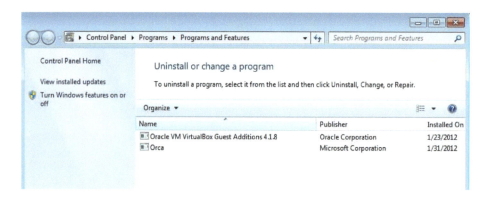

Now let's have a look at more details of the Windows Installer.

Components

Windows Installer **components** are parts of the software package like files, registry keys, shortcuts, etc.

Features

Windows Installer *features* are program units. These are optional parts of the program that a user installing that software can choose from: these may be help files, example data, plug-ins for the program and so on. These options are often displayed in a tree branch manner in the installer wizard: "parent" parts of the program have "children"; the "children" are the sub features of each parent and can be optionally installed or left out.

Merge & Transform

The information stored in an MSI for its installation can be changed, and this is done with the help of **merges** and **transforms**.

A transform adds or changes these settings. A typical reason to do so may be to change the language of an installation from English to Spanish.

A database transform adds or replaces elements in the original database. For example, a transform can change all of the text in an application's user interface from French to English.

Transforms also can manipulate what an application will install or not; this can help you create a dynamic installation, letting you focus on the specific needs and scenarios of the target user or computer.

Merging is more of interest to software authors, not necessarily those in charge of distributing the software in the last stages. Essentially, the information stored in different software packages can be merged together into one.

To create a transform, or to basically peek at the insides of an msi, you can choose from many MSI editors from **ORCA** (a tool provided for free from Microsoft:[2]), **SuperOrca**[3] or **InstEd**[4].

Here an example of **Orca**, the Windows Installer file(s) editor.

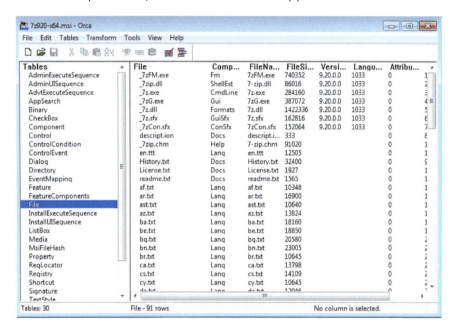

Picture 6 - The Orca Editor

Usage of Windows Installer

You can call the Windows Installer from the "Run" function in Windows or from a command line with "msiexec.exe". Typing "msiexec /?" will give you all available options:

---

[2] http://msdn.microsoft.com/en-us/library/windows/desktop/aa370557(v=vs.85).aspx)

[3] http://www.pantaray.com/msi_super_orca.html

[4] free version and priced advanced version: http://www.instedit.com/)

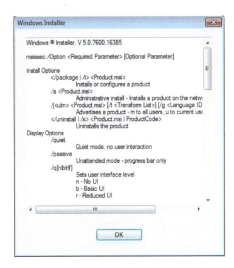

Picture 7 - The Windows Installer

Install Option

/I Installs a product with a wizard.

Example of 7Zip:

The free and open source archiver 7Zip is downloadable as a setup.exe and an MSI: we want to make things simple and thus use the MSI.

With the simple command: **msiexec.exe /i 7z920.msi /qb**

you can start the installation of 7Zip silently, displaying a basic interface.

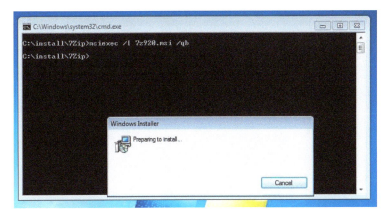

Picture 8 - Windows Installer in Silent / Basic mode

Dennis B. Waldon

Silent Mode Options

Using the **/q(n)** options with the msi.exe /I command lets you decide how much the User will see during the installation process. Here, two are mentioned:

/qn shows absolutely no User Interface.

/qb shows a basic User Interface.

Example of an installation with no wizard: **msiexec.exe /I yourApplication.msi /qn**

Update Options

Patches or updates in the form of a .msp file can also be applied with the Windows Installer. Using the **/update** option and the path of the update file will install that update.

Example msiexec.exe /p yourApplicationPatch.msp

Restart Options

Some applications require a reboot after installation. To either let the user decide if a reboot is ok or to postpone this reboot, the following options can be set:

/norestart tells the Installer to not reboot the machine, even if it is needed.

/promptrestart tells the Installer to ask the User to reboot when needed.

/forcerestart is the way to go to assure that a reboot is done, not giving the user a choice.

Example of a silent installation with no reboot:

yourApplication.msi /qn /norestart

Repair Option

/f Repairs a software package. This again has option parameters, like "a", to force all the files of an installation to be reinstalled.

Example of an installation repair:

msiexec.exe /f {85F4CBCB-9BBC-4B50-A7D8-E1106771498D} repairs the installation of Orca.

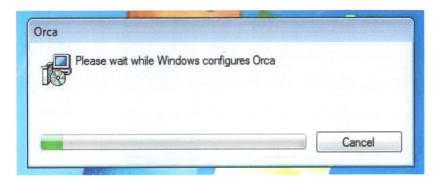

Picture 9 - Windows Installer Repair

Administrative Installation Option

/A creates an administrative installation. This simply decompresses and copies the package and its files to a folder of your choice. A file share on a network folder is a common example: installations on client machines can be run from there.

Uninstallation Option

/X uninstalls a software package. The *application ID* is needed. We give an example with the next part: Logging.

Dennis B. Waldon

Logging Option

/L sets the logging of the installer in motion. Added options like *i* logs status messages, *e* logs all error messages.

Example of a silent (basic GUI) uninstallation with a specified log file:

MsiExec.exe /X {85F4CBCB-9BBC-4B50-A7D8-E1106771498D} /L c:\install\orcafix.log /qb

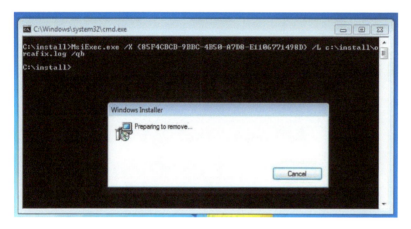

Picture 10 - Windows Installer uninstalling in Silent / Basic Mode

you can see here that the log file was created.

```
 Directory of C:\install

02/01/2012  03:00 PM    <DIR>          .
02/01/2012  03:00 PM    <DIR>          ..
02/01/2012  02:56 PM    <DIR>          orca
02/01/2012  03:02 PM            14,088 orcafix.log
               1 File(s)         14,088 bytes
               3 Dir(s)  11,104,505,856 bytes free
```

Picture 11 - The Windows Installer Log file

Here is the end of the log file: our product was successfully uninstalled.

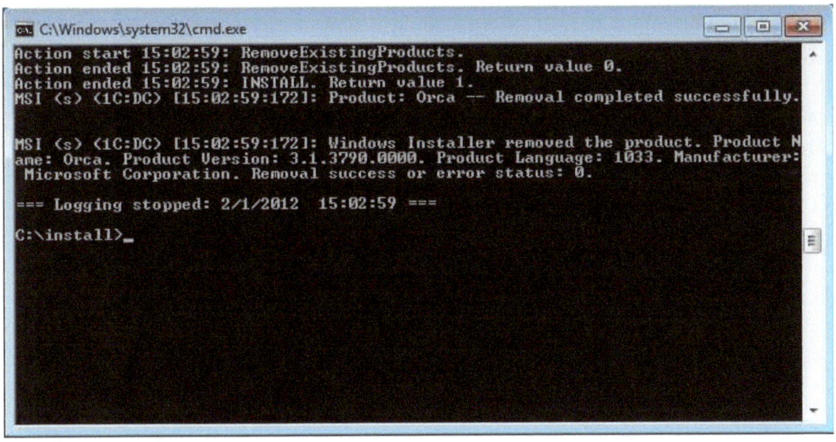

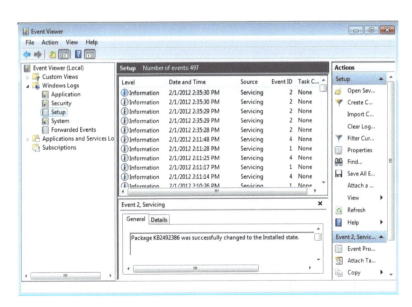

Picture 12 - Contents of the Installer Log

You will also be able to tell how the Windows Installer was successful or not by having a look at the event viewer. (type *eventvwr* at the command prompt).

Picture 13 - The Event Viewer

Dennis B. Waldon

Property

PROPERTY lets you pass values to the MSI. MSIs can be given variables and settings, and these values can be set when calling the Windows Installer and using the PROPERTY= option.

Have a look at the manufacturer's manual or support site for options their programs support.

TIP: Hidden MSIs

Sometimes, installers like to "hide" MSIs into a setup.

It is always a good thing to examine the installation program, especially if it is just one big file: most probably the setup.exe is just a "wrapper" for a MSI! Here is an example:

Example: Google SketchUp

Google SketchUp, a 3D designing program, is downloadable as a setup file.

If we take 7Zip, the free and very flexible archiver, we can look into the setup file, and...

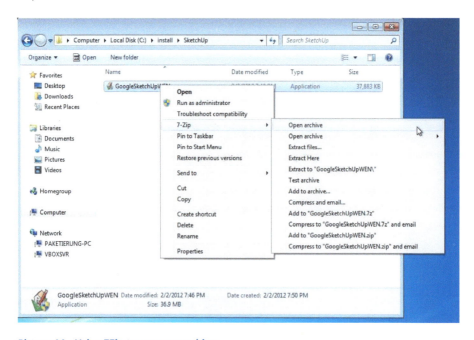

Picture 14 - Using 7Zip to open an archive

Voila! we find this: a MSI...

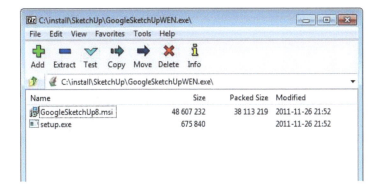

Picture 15 - The archive contents

that we can extract and later on distribute with all the goodies of Windows Installer.

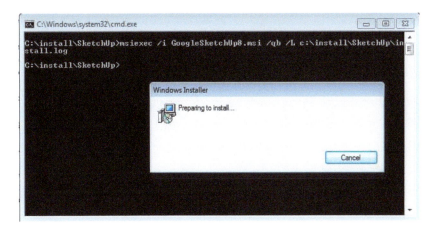

Picture 16 - Windows Installer Silent / Basic install

There are many more options to the Windows Installer; as mentioned, using the help function (**msiexec.exe /?**) will give you a list of all of them. Also, the Microsoft Web Site delivers complete documentation.[5]

---

[5] http://msdn.microsoft.com/en-us/library/windows/desktop/cc185688(v=VS.85).aspx)

Chapter 6: InstallShield

InstallShield (http://www.flexerasoftware.com/products/installshield.htm) is one of many software packaging tools. In essence (the complete functionality would be a book in itself), InstallShield tools help a developer bundle a software package all into a nice setup (the newer versions concentrate on MSI) that lets the user or administrator install the software both in a simple and more complex environment.

It comes in different editions from *Express* to *Premier*; all including different authoring tools for a programmer to make it easier for you to distribute their software. It brings an intelligence that can "just" install one application, or cover a "suite" of applications; automatically installing only those components that are needed in a given scenario.

Caution: InstallShield Setups can be "native" (containing only InstallShield mechanisms) or mixed with MSI installations (where commands are passed on to the Windows Installer).

When coming across an InstallShield setup, you have the following options of controlling what the setup.exe does:

Silent Installation
The option **/s** tells the InstallShield setup to install the program silently. This of course means that it has to be told what to do: where to install and how to install, and this is done beforehand with the help of a "recording" of how the software was installed. We will consider this in the next option **Record**.

Example: **setup.exe /s /f1"c:\install\app1\app1_setup.iss"**

Record

The option **/r** monitors the clicks and choices you make during the installation and writes them to a file called setup.iss (or whatever parameter you choose). By default it will be located in the Windows directory; if specified with the /f1 option it can be located at the path of your choice.

Example: **setup.exe /r /f1"c:\install\app1\app1_setup.iss"**

/f1 tells InstallShield to create the setup.iss file (the file where all the install actions are kept).

Logging

The Option **/f2** tells the InstallShield setup to log the progress of the installation. Especially when installing in silent mode, it would be helpful to know why a certain installation fails, because, as "silent mode" indicates, the user will not see that the installer is trying to do its job.

Example: **setup.exe /s /f2"c:\install\app1\app1_setup.log**

With the help of this log, you can find out if all went well, or by using the error codes that InstallShield writes into the log file, troubleshoot the installation.

Chapter 8: Portable Applications

Portable Applications are becoming more and more widespread: these are applications that are bundled in such a way that they can run stand-alone without installation. This is not to be confused with application virtualization (let's consider it as a close cousin; this will be covered in Chapter 10).

Definition.

Software may be deemed "portable" if its files can be copied anywhere and also started anywhere without installation. Oftentimes these programs are copied onto a USB drive and launched from there. That way, programs can be "carried" along without having to install them again and again on new clients the user may be working with.

Benefits.

It is worthwhile to put thought into using this technology:

- It's free (there are always exceptions to the rule)!
- It is very simple to deploy (almost zero installation effort)
- It does not leave a " footprint" (tell-tale marks of a program installation that still leaves "clutter" even though it was uninstalled).
- If there is a newer program version, just swap the file and / or directory. No installation!

Types of Portable Apps

Portable apps can be graphic editors, web design tools, internet browsers and tools, multimedia applications, office suites, programming environments and system tools.

"Installing" these programs is a simple copy of a file or directory, creating a link and you are basically ready to go.

Deploying Portable Apps

Scenarios of using Portable Apps:

- A dedicated directory on your freshly installed clients where the programs are located and launchable from the desktop or start menu

- Links on your desktop or start menu that start the program from a shared network drive

- Integration in your Software Deployment Suite: it downloads, decompresses the software into a directory of your choice and launches it from there.

This is an example of a desktop that uses shortcuts to Portable Apps that are in a dedicated directory on the hard drive.

None of these applications were installed in the classic sense, only copied into the directory and the links were copied for the user to start them.

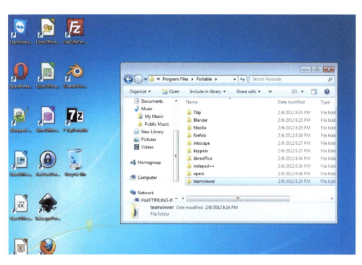

Picture 17 - A "Portable App" desktop!

You will receive some tips and tricks in deploying Portable Apps in Chapter 15.

Sources for Portable Applications

A good site to go looking for portable applications is http://www.portableapps.com, and even try the search engine of your choice if a portable version of your software is available.

Dennis B. Waldon

Chapter 9: Honorable Mentions

We have covered the 2 of the most widespread installers; there are many more, all with their strengths and weaknesses. A German saying goes: "All cook with water." Basically put, the principles for installers are all the same; its the user experience and additional functions that separate them.

There is a very interesting comment on unattended.sourceforge.net:

"To make an educated guess about how to run an installer unattended, you need to know which system was used to create it. Sometimes this will be obvious from the installer's splash screen; sometimes you can figure it out by running strings; and sometimes you will have to guess."[6]

You will most probably be able to tell what kind of installer you are dealing with by doing a trial run (installing it manually, and by the looks of the splash screen, or by looking at what the installer "dumps" into the TEMP directory of your system during the install). This can help in figuring out how to continue to later automate your installation).

Lets have a look at:

Installshield bundled together with MSI
You may come across an installer that has a classic "setup.exe", but launches an MSI; then of two possibilities are there to install silently or with other options.

1. Classic setup
This is a setup that we have discussed in the last chapter: "classic" parameters like **/s**, **/r** work for the installation.

Example: setup**.exe /s /f1c:\install\install01\setup.iss**

---

[6] http://unattended.sourceforge.net/installers.php

2. Basic MSI Setup

Basic MSI Setup means that the setup.exe needs to pass on parameters to the Windows installer.

Example: **setup.exe /s /v"/qn"**

This lets the setup.exe know to install silently, and to pass on the silent and no GUI parameter on to Windows installer.

Beware: Trial and Error! If at first you don't succeed, try, try again!

WISE Setups

Wise setups "tick" pretty much the same way as InstallShield but is a bit more limited with options.

Itninja.com[7] gives us a short table of how to use them:

Wise Setup.exe Switches

/T test mode

/X pathname extracts files into pathname

/Z pathname extracts files into pathname and reboots

/S silent install

/M prompts for windows, system, temp dirs

/M=filename specifies a value file similar to /d above,

but for standard variables

/M1 same as /m plus it prompts before any file that is self-registered

/M2 reserved for internal use by Wise during debugger sessions

---

[7] http://www.itninja.com

Dennis B. Waldon

Uninstall (Unwise.exe switches)

/Z remove empty directories, including one with unwise itself in it.

/A automatic mode, no user choices other than cancel.

/S silent mode, automatic mode with no user choices

/R rollback mode, selects option to rollback on uninstall

/U like automatic mode, but gives all choices other than custom/automatic

Inno Setup
Inno Setup[8] is a free installer for Windows systems. It can distribute on 32- and 64 bit systems and can be used to install with parameters[9].

/Silent or /VERYSILENT
with the /Silent option, a basic GUI is displayed to show progress, but nothing else.

With the /VERYSILENT option, nothing is displayed during installation.

/SUPPRESSMSGBOXES
This option hides and automatically answers questions raised by the installer. (Example: it automatically assumes "YES" to a request to keep newer files, or "NO" to confirm an overwrite.

/LOG or /LOG="FILENAME"
This tells the installer to create a log file in the TEMP directory of the user.

---

[8] http://www.jrsoftware.org/isinfo.php
[9] http://www.jrsoftware.org/ishelp/

If /LOG="FILENAME"; then you can specify where the installer should write the log file.

/NORESTART

This tells the installer to not reboot the system after an installation.

/LOADINF="FILENAME and /SAVEINF="FILENAME"

/Loadinf instructs the installer to use an "answer" file, which of course meant that an answer file has been created before using the /SAVEINF option.

/NOICONS

This instructs the installer to not create any start icons for the application (useful if you are using your own software deployment software and want to use your own links).

Nullsoft Scriptable Install System
This is a free, open-source installer[10].

/S Silent option
you can use the /S option to silently install.

/D Target Destination option
This option tells the installer to install to a specific directory other than standard.

_?=
This option uninstalls the program from the installed directory.

---

[10] http://nsis.sourceforge.net/Main_Page

AutoIT

AutoIT is not an installer; it is rather a powerful helper program that helps you automate tasks in Windows.

It has its own scripting language and can complete pre-recorded or scripted clicks, keyboard strokes and much more. It can run by itself (has no dependencies) and can even compile itself into an executable file that then executes itself automatically.[11]

---

[11] http://www.autoitscript.com/site/autoit/

Chapter 10: Application Virtualization

A giant leap in the last few years has been the development of *virtualizing applications*.

The thought behind this technology is to get rid of all those troublesome setups and dependencies, but to have one nice bundle that brings everything it needs with it. you could consider this application as an island: it has no connection with environment around it. It can be run just about anywhere, and it behaves as if it was installed in the classic way.

Imagine packaging an application -once-, and then deploying it to all necessary systems. your clients won't be changed in any way; and if the application has to change, just replace it after adding, removing or configuring it anew. you can have different versions of the same program running on the same system with no conflicts, as virtualized programs are all pretty much self-contained.

Benefits:

- Run old applications on newer systems
- No need of extra real or virtual machines that run the program
- Different versions of the same program can run on the same machine, maybe even at the same time; which is not really possible in the "classic" sense of installed applications.
- You are 100% sure that all clients in your system run the -exact- same software
- Faster deployment of programs (no setup needed)

The only issue is cost: good application virtualization is not necessarily cheap. There are free application virtualization tools out there, but since you are running business applications, you may need enterprise support and experience from a larger manufacturer.

Dennis B. Waldon

Virtualization Manufacturers

Manufactures you might want to have a look at:

AppZero[12], BoxedApp[13], Cameyo[14], Ceedo[15], Evalaze[16], InstallFree[17], Citrix XenApp[18], Novell ZENworks Application Virtualization[19], Endeavors Technologies Application Jukebox[20], Microsoft Application Virtualization[21], Spoon[22] and VMware ThinApp[23].

A further nice-to-have-heard of technique is application streaming: only the - parts- of a program you need are transferred to your client: this saves time, bandwidth. Check with the manufacturer if the virtualization implementation of their software supports this not utterly necessary, but nice-to-have feature.

Downside of application virtualization:

- Not all software packages can be virtualized. Some applications need specific hardware to run or software architectures that are not supported anymore or are just simply not possible to serve on a virtualized basis.[24]

---

[12] http:// www.appzero.com
[13] www.boxedapp.com
[14] www.cameyo.com
[15] www.ceedo.com
[16] http://www.evalaze.de/en/home/
[17] www.installfree.com
[18] www.citrix.com/XenApp
[19] www.novell.com/products/zenworks/applicationvirtualization
[20] www.numecent.com
[21] www.microsoft.com/systemcenter/appv/default.mspx
[22] spoon.net/
[23] www.vmware.com/products/thinapp/overview.html
[24] http://en.wikipedia.org/wiki/Application_virtualization

Part 3 - Install-It-yourself

This part is dedicated to operations you can use with tools you most probably already have: scripts and other tools.

Picture 18 - author / source: http://www.photocase.de/cydonna

Chapter 11: Install-It-yourself Part 1- Scripting:

Why use scripts?
Sometimes you will have certain tweaks or changes you want done to a system, but without having to trouble yourself with packaging, redistributing and the like.

Sometimes administrators have no other choice than scripting, due to lack of tools (and budget).

These scripts can be run on command, when a user logs in or logs off, and can even be timed with a scheduler.

Scripting is then the best way to go. With scripting, you can:

- easily move, copy & delete files and directories
- connect to network shares
- start & end programs

You can even create scripts that are even flexible in themselves, reacting on their environment, or create a user-driven interface that guides the script. Examples are given below.

Your choice of Scripting:
You have various methods and languages for creating scripts.

There are:

- Batch files (we will cover this in detail)
- Microsoft has released Power Shell[25], which is a powerful and flexible language to use
- VBScript[26] is another script language from Microsoft which lets you write scripts in a very flexible manner

---

[25] http://technet.microsoft.com/en-us/scriptcenter/dd742419
[26] http://en.wikipedia.org/wiki/VBScript

- Perl, Java, and much more are all possibilities to distribute and configure your environment automatically.

Scripting languages all have their syntax and are limited or more flexible in their possibilities: Batch programming is very simple, down-to-earth (it can get complex, but in itself it is a very simple language), and it is available on all Windows systems.

Other scripts need certain environments to run in and the syntax is not always so simple (especially for beginners), so that is why we will cover batch programming in this section.

Batch Files

Before we get into detail and into our first script, we want to spare a few thoughts regarding documentation. you will save yourself and fellow coworkers a lot of time and trouble with proper documentation.

A simple line covering an important section in your script goes a long way in helping you troubleshoot and understanding your code. you will come across scripts that you or someone else has worked on a long time ago, and simple and clear documentation will avoid much confusion.

REM is one of the commands you can use in your scripts at the beginning of each line of "comment" you leave in your script. Everything after a REM is ignored, the program "knows" that this is for "leave it out" code.

Batch files usually have the ending .bat or .cmd, so that the operating system knows that this is a file with commands it should run.

You can write a batch file with just about any editor; the Notepad program that comes with every Windows installation is perfect; open source programs like Notepad++[27] even help you with the code and highlights important parts of your script.

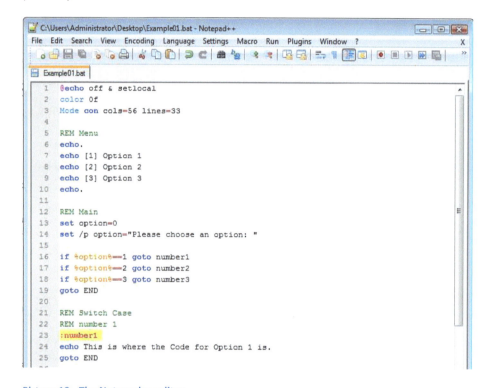

Picture 19 - The Notepad++ editor

Lets start with some basic vocabulary and examples.

27 http://notepad-plus-plus.org/

Useful commands for use in batch files

echo

"echo" tells your batch program to display something on your screen. As in our example before, we use the "echo" command to display options. By themselves they don't do anything yet, they are just a way to display the options to the user. (This could just as well be an announcement that something is going to happen, like: This is step 01 of 15").

The Code using "*echo*":

```
echo.
echo [1] Option 1
echo [2] Option 2
echo [3] Option 3
echo.

set option=0
set /p option="Please choose an option: "
pause
```

The Result:

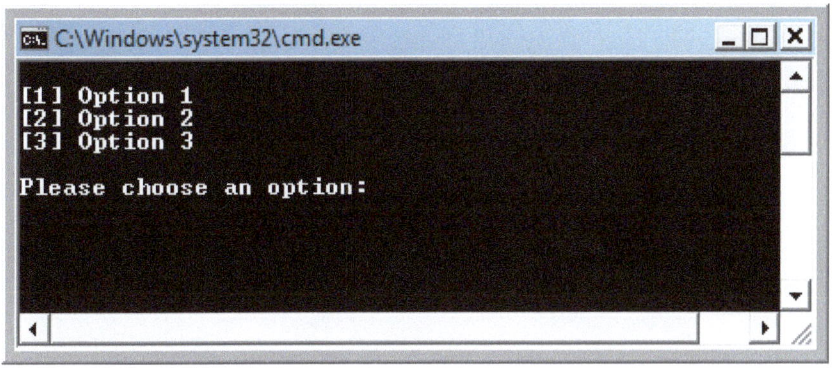

```
C:\Windows\system32\cmd.exe

[1] Option 1
[2] Option 2
[3] Option 3

Please choose an option:
```

Picture 20 - Script example output

If you use @echo off at the beginning of your script, the script will not display every command it executes. Otherwise your script will look like this:

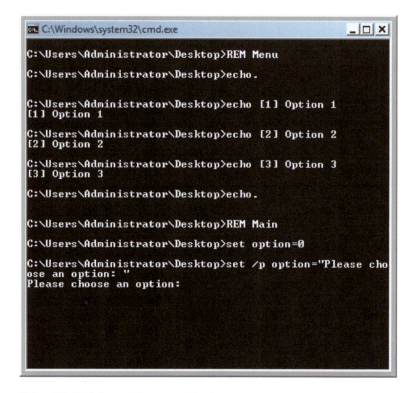

Picture 21 - Script example menu output

Pause

This almost goes without saying. It pauses your script until you press a button.

Sleep[28] is also a command to use, but has to be separately downloaded depending on your operating system version.

---

[28] http://www.microsoft.com/en-us/download/details.aspx?id=17657

If you do not want user interaction, but just for the script to wait n-seconds, you can use the following workaround: **PING**!

Ping is actually a tool to test network connectivity. you can "ping" a distant computer, and that computer, depending on the configuration, usually pings back.

To solve our problem of timing, your client can also ping itself. The workaround is to ping yourself n-number of times (one ping could be roughly estimated as 1 second), and however long you need your script to wait, you ping!

ping -n 10 localhost >nul

This will give you about 10s before your script continues. Raising the number will make the script wait longer.

xcopy

This is what you can use to copy files from A to B with control of how the copying is to be exactly done. This is actually an executable that Windows itself provides and offers a bit more functionality than the simple *copy* command. It can:

- check if files with the same name already exists and skip them
- copy files only with a certain attribute
- exclude files from copying
- it can distinguish between empty and full directories
- only copy the directories, and not the files themselves.

An example script could be:

```
@echo off
xcopy c:\test d:\test /E /Y
```

This little script copies everything from C:\test to d:\test, and answers every time a overwrite action is needed automatically with "yes".

set

This command lets you "declare" a variable or alias for use in your script. This saves time and reduces potential errors; the set command can be used to declare File paths for example.

```
@echo off & setlocal
set destination_path=c:\install\folder2
echo I will copy your files to %destination_path%
copy c:\install\folder1 %destination_path%
```

If you want to use Day, Month, or Year as variables, you can declare them this way:

```
set year=%date:~-4%
set month=%date:~3,2%
set day=%date:~0,2%
```

you can then use these variables in your commands. If you, say, want to create a directory based on the date the script is being executed, declare the variables we just mentioned and "fit" them into your command:

md c:\backup\%day%%month%%year%

This will created a directory with today's date.

The next chapter will review some variables that your operating system already has in store; you can use these as well to help you in your scripts.

goto

"Goto", as the name says, tells the program to "jump" to another part of the batch file.

you can declare various sections of your batch file by starting the line with ":"

As you have seen in our example above, we created a simple menu, and whatever choice the use makes, the batch file will jump to the section.

```
if %option%==1 goto number1
if %option%==2 goto number2
if %option%==3 goto number3
goto END

:number1
echo This is where the Code for Option 1 is.
goto END
:END
pause
```

This script, when told to either go to choice 1,2 or 3, will go to that specific section.

Section ":number1" then continues with the script with a "pause" command.

IF

IF is a practical way to check requirements first, and then continues on.

This example checks if a file exists (a log file from an installation). If it exists, it displays an error that this routine has been run before.

```
@echo off & setlocal
IF EXIST c:\install.log (
echo This installation has already been run!
) ELSE (
echo This program will now proceed with installation.
)
pause
```

...or it can be used to dynamically jump to another section:

Dennis B. Waldon

```
@echo off & setlocal
IF EXIST c:\install.log (
echo This installation has already been run!
) ELSE (
goto INSTALL
)
:INSTALL
echo The setup will now start silently
```

Redirection

you can "redirect" output of a command into a file, which is nothing other than a log file.

A simple command like:

dir > log.txt will write the output of the dir (list directory contents) command into the log.txt.

```
27.01.2012  15:26  <DIR>      Folder1
27.01.2012  15:26  <DIR>      Folder2
27.01.2012  15:26  <DIR>      Folder3
27.01.2012  15:26  <DIR>      Folder4
```

Another useful example, which writes the error right into an error.log along with date and time:

@echo off & setlocal

```
IF EXIST c:\install.log (
echo This installation has already been run! > error.log
) ELSE (
goto INSTALL
)
:INSTALL

date /T > install.log
time /T >> install.log

echo This program will now proceed with installation >> install.log
```

Notice the double ">": this tells the batch program to ADD content to the file, otherwise it would replace everything in the file.

Call

The command "call" tells your batch file to "call" or open another batch file. When this batch file is completed and ends itself, the starting batch file will continue. The script example

call step01.bat

will call the step01.bat, wait till completion, and then continue.

This is helpful if you want to have your scripting more modular outside of one single batch file.

Stop a running process: TASKKILL

taskkill stops a running process (this is often necessary to make sure the same program is not running).

taskkill /IM process.exe /F

The **/IM** lets you give this command the Name of the process you want to "kill" (notepad.exe, for example) and the /F forces this if necessary.

Start or Stop a Windows Service

With the help of "net stop" or "net start" (which has dozens of uses; you can see them if you type "net /?"), we can stop or start Windows services. This example stops the DNS Client Service that you would see in the Services component in your control panel. (Note that if the service name has blanks, envelope the service name with "")

net stop dns-client

We can also use the "**sc**" command. Type "**sc /?**" in the command prompt to find out all the options.

Using the "sc" plus the name of the service, you can stop or start a service from the command prompt.

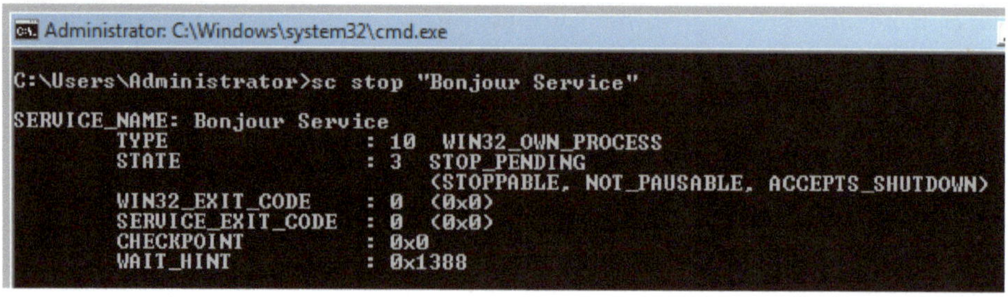

Picture 22 - Stopping a service with sc.exe

To log what happened (or sometimes didn't), you can redirect everything into a log file, using the example we had before:

sc stop *service name* > c:\test\stop_services.log

Start and Wait

The command "start" will start a program, and the **/wait** parameter tells the program to wait until the process is done until moving on. Otherwise your batch will run from line to line and start everything as fast as it can. Caution: setup programs sometimes "spawn" (create new process that run independently) and then close themselves, leaving the spawned process to complete installation. Windows or your batch file will not necessarily notice this.

Shutting Down / Rebooting

The "shutdown" command can shutdown your computer or reboot it, along with parameters like how long it should wait, if it is to force a shutdown, etc.

shutdown -f -r -t 15

Tells the computer to forcefully reboot and not to wait for programs if they do not shut down properly (**-f and -r**), and sets the time to 15 seconds (-t 15)

Chapter 12: Understanding variables

Variables are there to help programmers save time and avoid error. A variable is a value that you can give to a certain "placeholder": that placeholder can then be inserted almost anywhere later anywhere, and your programming environment will know what to substitute it with.

Why use variables?

Hard-Code vs. Variables.

There are two ways you can deal with recurring objects when programming or calling functions in a system:

Hard Code.

You can "hard-code", meaning that you type the full path, full name or whatever object you are calling each and every time you need it.

This is time-consuming and prone to error especially with longer names. The other downside to hard-coding is that it is not necessarily flexible across systems. Take operations that involve the user's name. Hard-coding force you to implicitly specify the user in your script. Which means that you would have to re-write the script to run for another user? Using the variable %username% will automatically fill out the user name for you.

Variables.

The other option is to use variables. Let us use a similar example to the above-mentioned.

Removing a link from the "**all users**" profile (the place where settings for all users on a given system are given) could be removed by using the hard-coded way (which would only work with some versions of Windows):

del C:\Documents and Settings\All Users\Startmenu\New Document.lnk or used with the variable:

del %allusersprofile%\startmenu\New Document.lnk (which will work with almost all Windows versions

Using System Variables

On the following page we want to show you a table of some variables that can make your life a whole lot easier.

Variable	Windows XP	Windows Vista/7
%ALLUSERSPROFILE% and %PROGRAMDATA%	C:\Documents and Settings\All Users	C:\ProgramData
%APPDATA%	C:\Documents and Settings\{username}\Application Data	C:\Users\{username}\AppData\Roaming
%COMPUTERNAME%	{computername}	{computername}
%COMMONPROGRAMFILES%	C:\Program Files\Common Files	C:\Program Files\Common Files
%COMMONPROGRAMFILES(x86)%	C:\Program Files (x86)\Common Files	C:\Program Files (x86)\Common Files
%COMSPEC%	C:\Windows\System32\cmd.exe	C:\Windows\System32\cmd.exe
%HOMEDRIVE%	C:	C:
%HOMEPATH%	\Documents and Settings\{username}	\Users\{username}
%LOCALAPPDATA%		C:\Users\{username}\AppData\Local
%LOGONSERVER%	\\{domain_logon_server}	\\{domain_logon_server}
%PATH%	C:\Windows\system32;C:\Windows;C:\Windows\System32\Wbem;{plus program paths}	C:\Windows\system32;C:\Windows;C:\Windows\System32\Wbem;{plus program paths}
%PATHEXT%	.COM;.EXE;.BAT;.CMD;.VBS;.VBE;.JS;.WSF;.WSH	.com;.exe;.bat;.cmd;.vbs;.vbe;.js;.jse;.wsf;.wsh;.msc
%PROGRAMDATA%		%SystemDrive%\ProgramData
%PROGRAMFILES%	%SystemDrive%\Program Files	%SystemDrive%\Program Files
%PROGRAMFILES(X86)%	%SystemDrive%\Program Files (x86) (only in 64-bit version)	%SystemDrive%\Program Files (x86) (only in 64-bit version)
%PROMPT%	Code for current command prompt format. Code is usually PG	Code for current command prompt format. Code is usually PG
%PSModulePath%		%SystemRoot%\system32\WindowsPowerShell\v1.0\Modules\
%PUBLIC%		%SystemDrive%\Users\Public
{Drive}:\$Recycle.Bin	C:\Recycle.Bin	C:\$Recycle.Bin
%SystemDrive%	C:	C:
%SystemRoot%	The Windows directory, usually C:\Windows, formerly C:\WINNT	%SystemDrive%\Windows
%TEMP% and %TMP%	%SystemDrive%\Documents and Settings\{username}\Local Settings\Temp	%SystemDrive%\Users\{username}\AppData\Local\Temp
%USERDOMAIN%	{userdomain}	{userdomain}
%USERDATA%	%SystemDrive%\Documents and Settings\{username}	%SystemDrive%\Users\{username}
%USERNAME%	{username}	{username}
%USERPROFILE%	%SystemDrive%\Documents and Settings\{username}	%SystemDrive%\Users\{username}
%WINDIR%	C:\Windows	C:\Windows

29

---

[29] http://en.wikipedia.org/wiki/Environment_variable

Dennis B. Waldon

Using your own variables.

With the command "**set**" you can define your own variables.

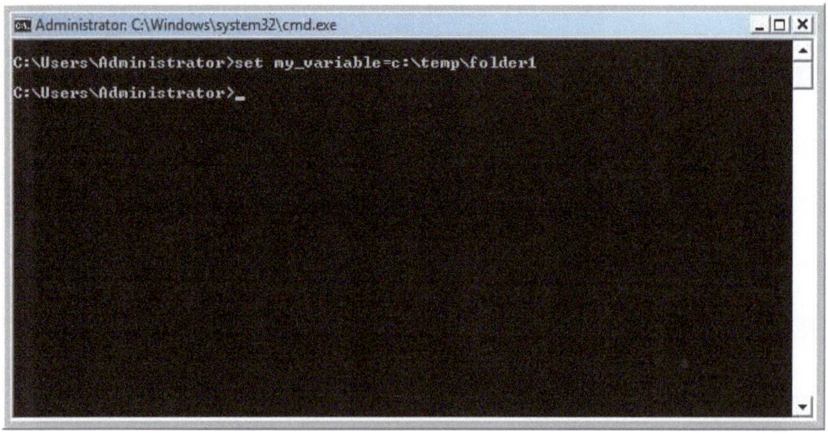

Picture 23 - Setting a variable

and with a simple "**set**" command you can see your variable displayed:

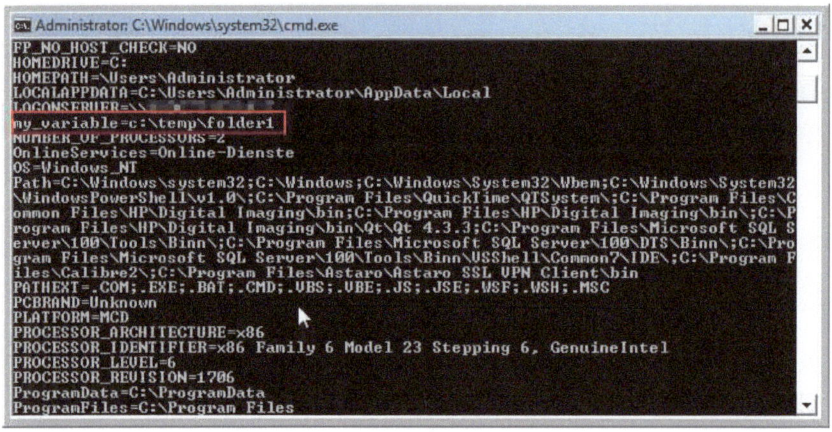

Picture 24 - The set variable

Chapter 13: Install-It-yourself Part 2- Repackaging:

Repackaging is the process of "snapshotting" or "capturing" an installation for your own redistribution in the future. This involves recording an installation: a scan of your system is made before the installation and after. The difference between the two is your snapshot, or capture of the installation.

Why do this?

- You may want to create your own distribution of files without buying a Software Authoring tool.

- You may choose to customize an installation: adding things like additional files, shortcuts or settings can be "snuck" into the new redistributable package and installed in all future installations.

- Some software setups simply don't allow for a silent or automated installation. your capture lets you turn such an installation into an automatic, redistributable and configurable one.

Downside: you have to be really careful with recapturing software because:

- Any other programs running at the same time create files and "manipulate" the system that is being monitored. These changes flow into your recording, and sifting these out can be a challenge. Programs like antivirus scanners, Windows Update are prime examples.

- Some Installers, as mentioned before, check the environment and thus dynamically install or update components on your system. Example: If a certain component is already installed, it may skip that part of the installation. After recording , repackaging and deploying on a system that is different, this can cause a non-functional program, and now its up to you to find out why (the environment check the original installer did was left out, and the component install or upgrade wasn't done).

Steps to "sanitize" your environment

To make sure your system is only running the absolute necessary, use this simple checklist:

Services

Are only the important services running, and the rest left out? Windows has dozens of services running, and you may not know each and every one of them, but services like Windows Update, Antivirus Scanners and the like are best stopped or disabled.

To see what services are running on your lab machine, to stop them or configure their status, type "services.msc" in the Windows Run prompt (Use Windows Key + R).

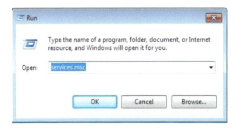

Picture 25 - The command window

Here is the list of all services on a given machine.

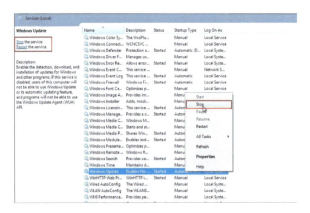

Picture 26 - Windows services

It is best to disable the ones you know and don't need. This is done via "properties".

Processes

With a simple CTRL+ALT+DEL you can see what programs are running in the background, and end them there.

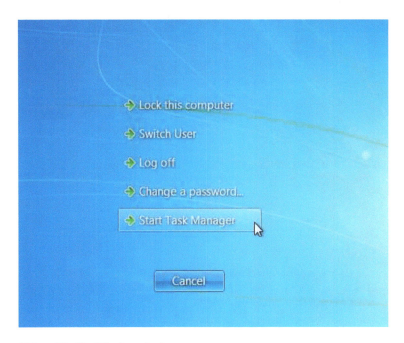

Picture 27 - The Windows Lock screen

After CTRL+ALT+DEL, this is an example screenshot of the list of programs running in the background:

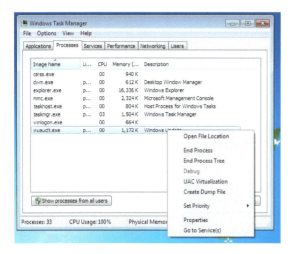

Picture 28 - Stopping a running process with task manager

No other unnecessary software installed

Have as few installed programs on your machine as possible. Even if they are not running, they can influence what an installer does and does not do!

Repackaging - a quick and dirty How-To.

We want to consider the free and easy repackaging tool from ITNinja.com[30].

This program will create a snapshot of our system, let us install the program we want to package, and then write everything into a nice and compact MSI file for easy distribution in the future.

Remember: only repackage if you really have to. Installers usually bring all necessary "equipment" and intelligence on board to install their programs. Repackaging may "overlook" some procedures that an installer doesn't, and the result can be a non-working or faulty program installation.

Running a Repackager

---

[30] http://www.itninja.com

Lets get started with repackaging software! In this case we want to use the AppDeploy Repackager from ITNinja.com.[31]

The AppDeploy Repackager has two basic functions: creating project files based on a system snapshot and the creation of a project file and Windows Installer setup.

What does it do and not do[32]?

What it can do:

- It performs a snapshot of the file and registry systems before and after an installation is performed in order to determine the intended changes of the setup being repackaged
- An exclusion list is included, and may be easily updated, to automatically disregard desired folders and registry items
- The exclusion list feature offers a description field so you can document such items.
- It generates a shareable project file
- It generates an MSI setup (based on the contents of the project file)
- The tool can create a MSI

What it cannot do:

- It does not include the ability to view or edit an MSI file
- It handles only file and registry data. Therefore more complex setups requiring the following may fail to perform as expected:
- Services
- Device drivers
- Environment variables

---

[31] http://www.itninja.com/link/download-the-appdeploy-repackager

[32] http://www.itninja.com/blog/view/appdeploy-repackager-frequently-asked-questions

Also note that the file and registry is saved during initial and second snapshots. These saved copies are what is used to determine changes (comparison is not done against the live file system or registry). Processing of DLL's and ActiveX object that can not be identified via registry or file system changes may result in registration issues.

A repackage scenario and How-to:

There are "classic" scenarios of simple applications you can repackage, but lets say you want wrap several different applications into one installation.

All roads lead to Rome, and you will always get different opinions on how and what to package. In this scenario, I thought of a special "construction", just so you get the feel of what is possible. It definitely is not the "recommended" method, but you will see what I mean to show with this example.

There are pros and cons to this example scenario, but its up to you how you want to do it. (These programs even have a silent install option, but I still want to wrap it up into one installation).

Let's say you want to install a "minimalist" installation of Notepad++[33], an image viewer like Irfanview[34], and then install the plugins for Irfanview. In a nutshell, the instructions on how to start a repackaging would be:

---

[33] http://notepad-plus-plus.org/
[34] http://www.irfanview.com/

1. Start the AppDeploy Repackager & choose to start a new project based on system changes

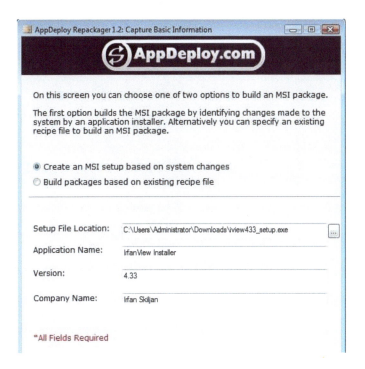

Fill out the forms with the following information:

- Where the setup file location is
- The name you would like to give the application
- The Version of the software setup
- The company name.

In this case, let's start the install of Irfanview first.

2.   In the next step, include or exclude directories for the Repackager.

you can leave the standard mode, or go into more detail with the "advanced" option.

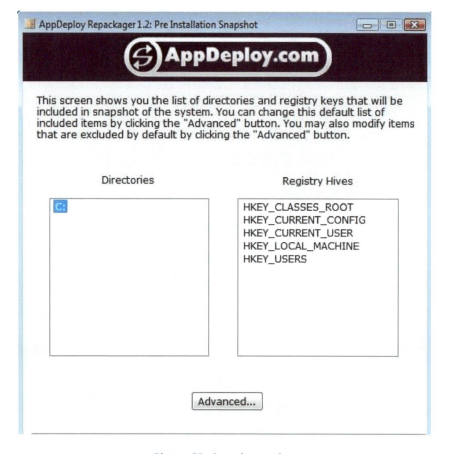

Picture 30 - Snapshot settings

3. ***Let the Repackager create the "snapshot" of your system.***

It basically scans a before- and after-image of the installation. This may take a while.

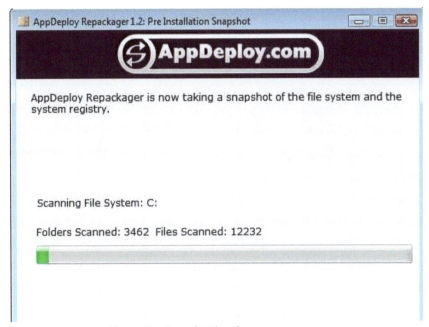

Picture 31 - Snapshotting the system

4. ***Now you the installation can be started.***

Once the first installation is complete, **do not end**! We are going to do some work "behind the scenes".

Dennis B. Waldon

Picture 32 - The installation launch

We are installing Irfanview. For demonstration purposes, let's leave the desktop icons option, but remove them manually later.

Picture 33 - The IrfanView installation window

70

5. *Don't let the Repackager scan just yet!*

Let's install the plugins and Notepad++ in the background. Then, lets delete the desktop icons.

Picture 34 - Icons on the desktop from the setup

Now we can start the software scanning.

Picture 35 - Taking the after-snapshot

The Repackager shows us a list of files it has marked as new since the first scan. you can uncheck files and registry settings you may not want to be included.

Be aware! Repackage on a clean machine with as little as possible running!

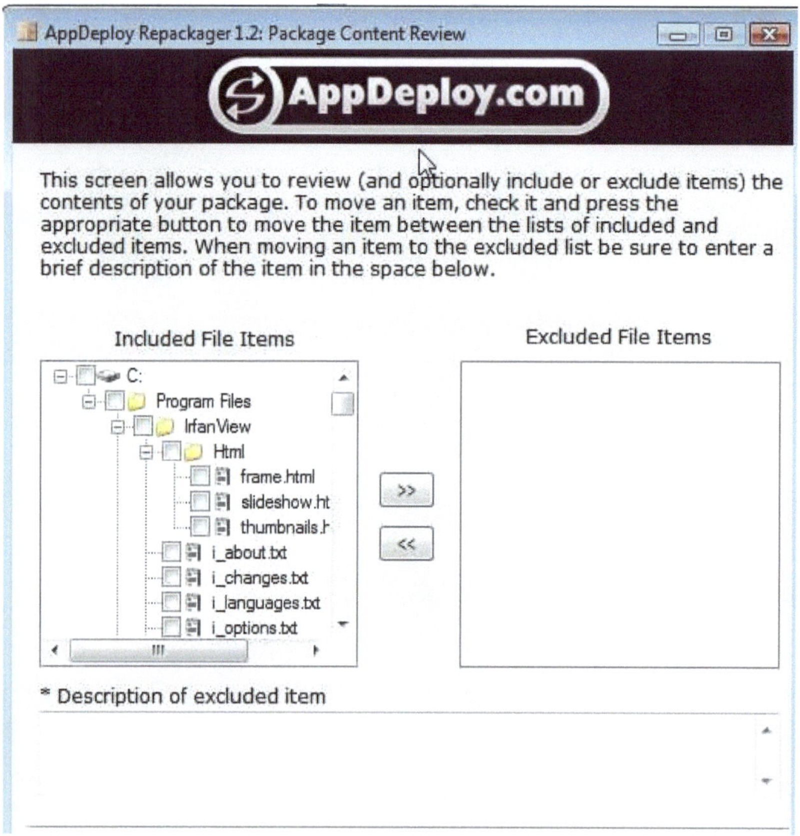

Picture 36 - Exclusion window

6. Create the MSI.

Fill out the following information:

- The icon you want to use for the installation

- Destination of the "recipe" file a name (an xml file where all the recorded changes are kept)

- A name for the MSI. The MSI file will then be located where you specified in the wizard.

The MSI is being created.

Picture 38 - Creation of the MSI

Voila! The MSI file is ready for deployment.

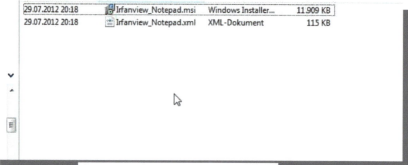

Picture 39 - The created MSI and XML file

7. *Save and Test*

Save the MSI, and on a clean machine install the MSI and check if everything runs smoothly.

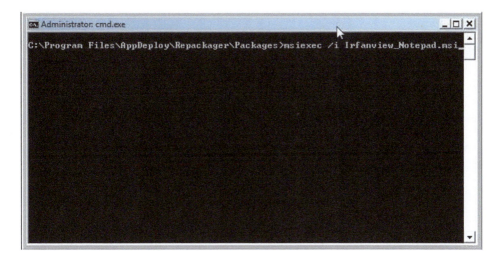

Picture 40 - Testing the MSI on a clean machine via command line

8. *Just to mention...*

Ninite.com is a website that offers to package together a large amount of well-known applications into one executable.

Programs like Google Chrome, Firefox, Skype, Winamp, Flash, iTunes, Open Office and the like can be grouped into one simple installation file that downloads the newest version of each and installs them. Available in a free and professional version.

http://ninite.com/

Chapter 14 - The Clean Machine

For every packaging or repackaging purpose, a "clean" machine, or one that is as close to the real environment but without too many strings attached is very, very important!

Most of the time you will need several tests with each package of software: once to see how it "ticks", and then to experiment with the installation and then tweaking it.

Almost every installation leaves what we could call "residue": things that lie in the system in the form of files or settings that are not necessarily uninstalled with the uninstallation process.

In essence, once your system has been touched with an installation, it cannot be considered "clean" anymore: behavior can be very different the next time the installer is run.

Lab tests with real hardware

One can set up a test lab with real pcs; the downside of doing this is that it is relatively difficult to "revert" this machine to a clean state. There are imaging software suites out there, but imaging and restoring are a time-consuming process.

That is why we suggest using virtual machines.

Lab tests with Virtual Machines

Virtual machines are operating systems that run "on top" of another operating system.

The computer running the virtualization software is the "host", and the operating system running is the "guest". Another way to describe it: Virtualization lets you treat an operating system like an application. It runs inside its own little box, and basically "believes" it is running on a stand-alone machine.

The Benefits:
Benefits of doing this?

- reduce hardware costs (you can have several virtual machines running on one host
- faster recovery and imaging process (use of "snapshots": we will discuss this later on)
- it is the simplest way to keep a flexible lab environment.

There are several virtualization software manufacturers: VMware[35] is one, Virtual Box[36] is an alternative, cost-free alternative. For general use in packaging and deployment, Virtual Box is the quick, easy and cost-free way to go. VMware is a powerful tool with many further possibilities, but it comes with a price tag.

In our scenario, we will discuss Virtual Box.

---

[35] http://www.vmware.com
[36] http://www.virtualbox.org

Dennis B. Waldon

Virtual Box - in a nutshell

As you can see in the screenshot below, Virtual Box lets you install various operating systems into a virtualized environment.

These are "machines" that have hard disks, network cards, memory, the works; only *virtually*.

The components for the virtual machine itself are "real", and can almost be treated 1:1 with a real environment. Virtual machines generally need less RAM than real ones would.

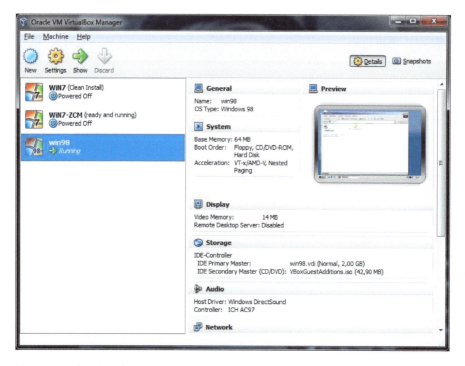

Picture 41 - The VirtualBox application

More than one virtual machine can be run at the same time: the only limit is the processing and memory power of your host.

Flexibility and speed: Cloning and Snapshotting

A virtual machine is actually just a set of files on your host. Thus, there are more things that you can do relatively faster with a virtual machine than with a real machine.

The main functions we want to introduce are:

- Creating machines very fast
- Cloning
- Snapshotting

Dennis B. Waldon

Creating a virtual machine.

If you have installed Virtual Box, click on the "new" button and the wizard asking you for the settings, step-by-step, will start.

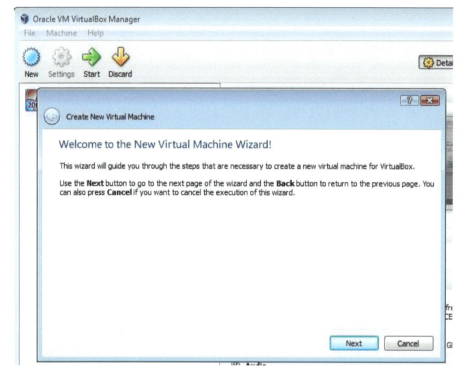

Picture 42 - The virtual machine wizard

The wizard will ask you for a name for the virtual machine, and what type of operating system it will be.

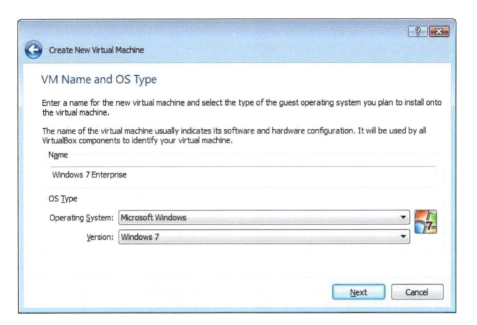

Picture 43 - Selecting the guest operating system

The next step will be to allocate memory to your virtual machine. As mentioned, virtual machines can work smoothly with less virtual RAM than real ones, so experiment here. you can fairly trust the suggestions Virtual Box gives you.

Dennis B. Waldon

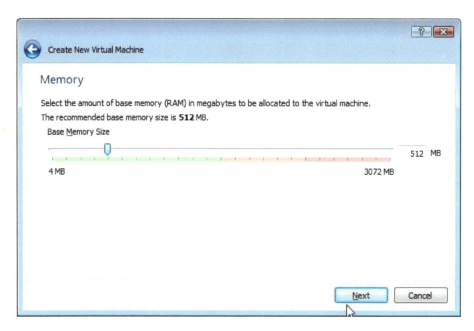

Picture 44 - Memory settings

Now you will be asked to created a virtual hard disk. This is the file the system will be installed into.

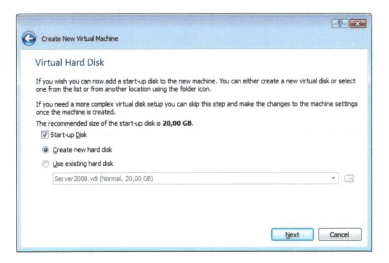

Picture 45 - Virtual Harddisk settings

Virtual Box will ask you the format of the virtual disk file. you can keep the standard image; only if you are thinking of "transporting" this image later or using it with another virtualization software you can decide on a different format.

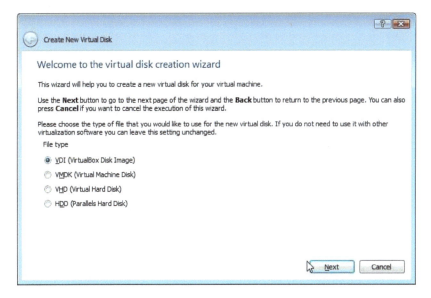

Picture 46 - Virtual Harddisk type settings

Virtual Box also want so know if you want the disk to be a fixed size, or if it should be able to "grow" with time. We recommend to "dynamically allocated" size (letting it grow as necessary), as the disk will be kept as small as possible at the beginning, yet can grow with size when necessary.

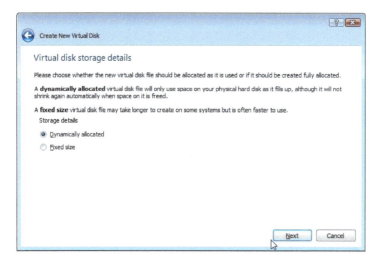

Picture 47 - Size allocation of a virtual disk

You can decide on where to save the virtual machine's files on the host.

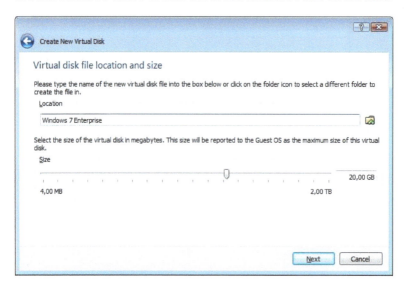

Picture 48 - Virtual disk location and size

At the end of your creating your virtual machine, a summary is displayed.

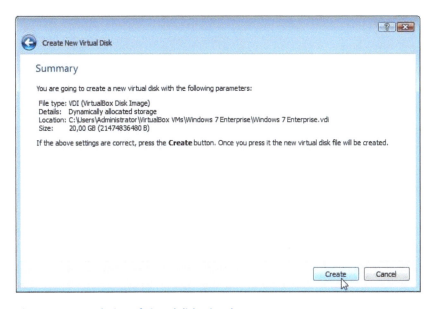

Picture 49 - Completion of virtual disk wizard

Start / Stopping a virtual machine

With the help of the Virtual Box graphical user interface (GUI), you can start, stop and pause (!) a virtual machine.

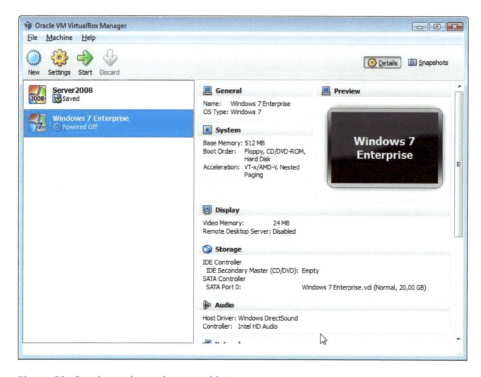

Picture 50 - Starting and stopping a machine

Starting a VM (virtual Machine) for the first time.
The first time you start a VM, the wizard will tell you about the Auto Capture feature.

Virtual Box needs to know how you want to handle the mouse when working with the guest system. When you move the mouse around the host, Virtual Box will "release" the mouse for use.

When the mouse is moved over the virtual machine area, it "captures" the mouse for use in the VM. If somehow the mouse gets "stuck" in the virtual machine and can't be used outside the Virtual Box window, the standard key RIGHT CTRL will tell Virtual Box to release it.

Picture 51 - Key capture dialog

Once your machine is installed, it is recommended to install the virtual machine add-ons.

These are specific drivers and "helpers" to run your machine properly in a virtual environment.

you will need these Additions to be able to move folders to and from your machine (will be considered later in this chapter).

Dennis B. Waldon

Picture 52 - Installing Guest Addition Part 1

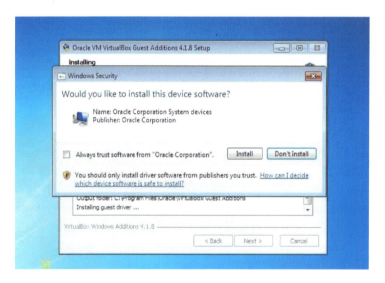

Picture 53 - Installing Guest Additions Part 2

Getting Files into and out of your machines - Sharing Folders

you may want to get files into or out of your VM. One way to do this is to use the "Shard Folders" option in Virtual Box.

The idea behind this is to create a network share in your virtual machine which is a folder on your host. you can copy files into this folder, and they will be available to both guest and host.

CAUTION! Guest Additions have to be installed!

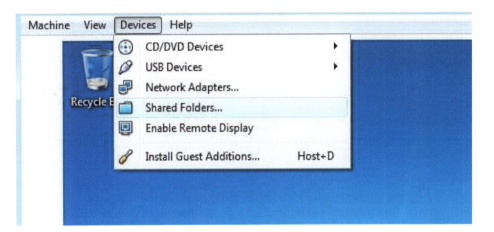

Picture 54 - Sharing folders

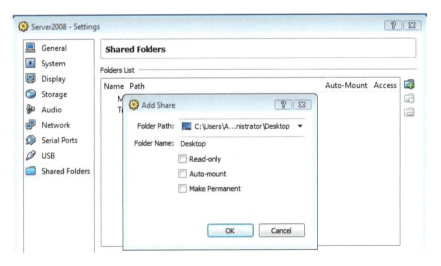

Picture 55 - Shared folder location

Hold it right there: Snapshots.

Definition.

Snapshots are one of THE finger-licking benefits of virtualization.

you can more or less save the *complete* machine in a certain state, continue on with whatever your heart desires with, and if you want to get back to that specific state in time, presto! Load that snapshot and you are back where you were.

Such things were only possible with tedious imaging of real computers, which required space and lots of time. With snapshotting, all it involves is a matter of seconds.

Case in point.

you can now save the state of the machine, say, before you install Microsoft Office. After snapshotting, tinker around with the software installation as you wish.

If something went wrong, or if you want to do the same installation again but just a bit different on a machine that is "clean" (once you installed something on your machine, technically you cannot call it "clean" anymore), just revert to that snapshot and you are good to go.

How-to.

Click on "**Machine - Take Snapshot**" or right-click on the machine and choose this option.

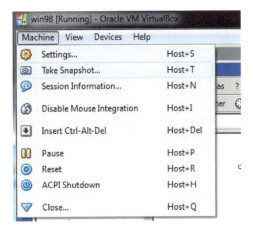

Picture 56 - Taking a Snapshot

Virtual Box will ask you for a name for this snapshot: give it something meaningful like: "Clean without any programs" or "Office installation with no patches".

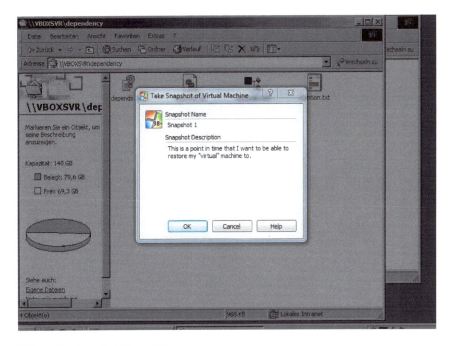

Picture 57 - Snapshot description

Dennis B. Waldon

If you click on "Snapshots" on your far right, you will see all the snapshots, or machine states in time. you can then easily jump back and forth to a point in time of what your installation looked like.

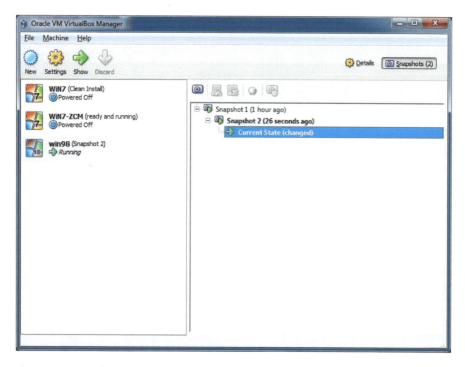

Picture 58 - Snapshot overview in VirtualBox

Cloning virtual machines.

Definition.

Cloning helps you create virtual machines - really fast, on the basis of an already existing machine.

If you just want to have another machine with the same installation prerequisites, then cloning is the way to go.

Case in point.

Choose "**Machine - Clone**" (or press **CTRL+O**, or right-click the virtual machine) within the Virtual Box Manager after highlighting the machine you would like to clone.

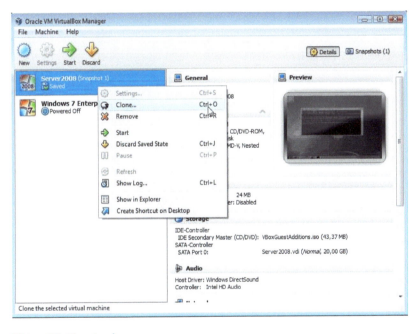

Picture 59 - How to clone

you will then be greeted by the Cloning Wizard!

The first step of the cloning wizard is to give your new machine a name. you will also have the option to give your machine a new MAC Address (a number that is unique for every network card).

In this case, a new MAC address is reasonable, as we don't want to have any network issues.

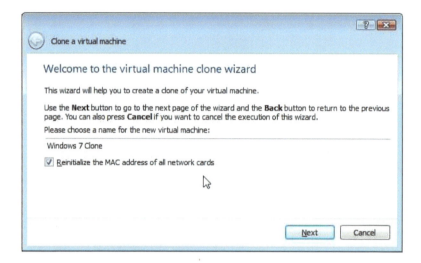

Picture 60 - The cloning wizard

We then can choose from a **_full clone_** or a **_linked clone_**. A full clone is a complete copy of the machine and its files. A linked clone creates a new machine, but keeps the original files, and saves all further changes into this machine. (saves space, but can get hairy when trying to delete virtual machines that are linked).

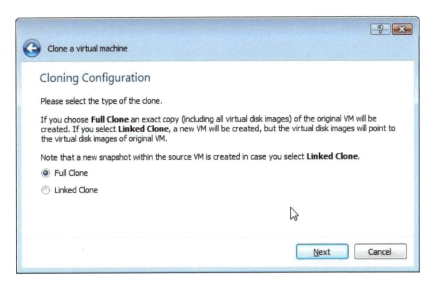

Picture 61 - Cloning Type

The next thing the wizard asks of you is if you want to clone the current state of the machine, or all snapshots of the system. your decision! In this case we cloned a machine in the current state, as it is in a state where we just want it as a baseline for further clones.

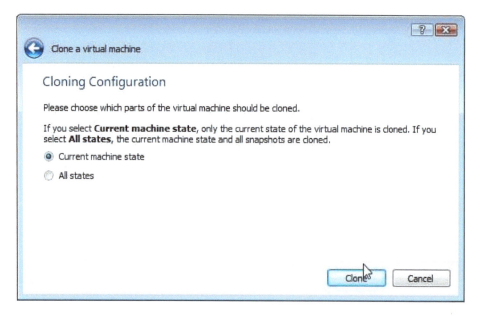

Picture 62 - Cloning from a state

This starts the cloning process: a new machine, based completely on the old, is on its way. This operation can take a while depending on your system.

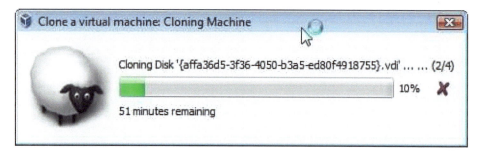

Picture 63 - Cloning can take some time

Part 4 - Documentation, Packaging and Deployment

The following 3 chapters cover the aspects of correct documentation (helps you in the long run!), how to distribute software packages using various methods and a special peek at a software management suite: Novell ZenWorks Configuration Management.

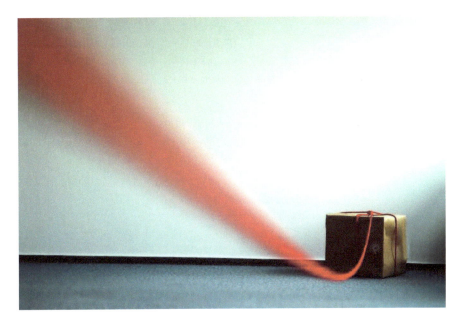

Picture 64 - http://www.photocase.de/kallejipp

Chapter 15 - Document, Package & Deploy!

Now we are getting closer and closer to the end of this book, and hopefully your fingers are twitching to get working! But first, another word concerning...

Documentation!
Document, document, document! We know. They know it. We ALL know. We need to document, and if already document, document a bit *more*.

Make your life and those of your workmates easier! It takes more time to find out how you did something later on than documenting those few lines for each piece of software you prepare and deploy. A simple table with headers like Name, Manufacturer, Support Website & Version is the least we should do.

The four areas we want to see documented should be:

1. Preparation.
2. Installation.
3. Launch.
4. Uninstallation.

Preparation.
- Notes and observations about what trouble one may came across when installing the "normal" way *and* silently.
- Document links to support sites and forums.

Installation.

- What parameters are needed to start the installation process?
- Are any "helper" tools needed for the installation (archiver with command line to unzip, scripts for installation steps, etc.).
- What has to be done to "clean up" after the installation process (removal of links, temporary files, files needed for installation).

Launch.

- What kind of links are needed to start the program / program suite?
- What parameters are needed to launch the program?

Uninstallation.

- What has to be done to uninstall the program?
- What files have to be removed manually ("left-overs" from the uninstaller?)
- Are there any registry settings or files or directories that could conflict with future re-installations?

Packaging!

All right!

Overview of installers - check!

A machine to test deploy / repackage - check!

Now just a few tips and tricks for packaging that nice little program you are itching to get rolled out.

Tips and Tricks for packaging.

Where, o where will your software be?

you basically have 3 choices of where your software will be stored and reachable for your clients to deploy:

Shared drive.

A shared drive with subdirectories for each package is one of the best ways clients can reach the packaged files. This could be a dedicated drive letter that all clients map when logging in.

A note on Security.

To avoid everyone being able to reach everything, consider doing the following:

- Create a group for each application (maybe one with the name of the application with a prefix like "app_") in your directory service (Active Directory, eDirectory,...).
- Set rights to the subfolders and only give the appropriate rights for this folder to this group.
- Add users to these groups when they need the application.

Why?

- This will avoid the user being "swamped" with directories, should he or she wander to this network share.
- Only users that are allowed to have certain programs will be able to install them.
- Adding a user to a group automatically gives him or her all the rights needed.
- Login scripts and the like can be used to perform certain actions based on these groups, and you will not have to configure dozens of users manually.

Locally.

When rolling out a client, many companies install the main programs and their installers locally on the drive, and let the installer call the packages from there.

Many software distribution suites also do this: when installing, they first copy the needed files to the local disk and start the installation from there. At the end of the installation, the files are either left there for repair or reinstallation procedures in the future, or erased.

A big help for saving space is to compress these files when unneeded: programs like 7Zip come with a command line option that can easily be fitted into scripts.

With a simple line like:

c:\install\program01\7zr.exe x -y c:\install\program01\compressedfiles.7z

one can easily deflate downloaded, compressed files automatically, and then delete the files or the compressed image after installation.

These files can also be copied from a network share and then decompressed locally; this saves bandwidth and processing time.

Software Deployment Suites

Software deployment suites like ZenWorks Configuration Management let you "upload" your installation files, set the actions you want to take when installing, launching and uninstalling this package, and it will automatically download these files to your client and complete the mentioned actions.

We will have a look at this management suite later on as one example of many suites.

Deploy!

Now we are finally at the part of deploying. It was a long road, but we hoped to have made it interesting!

There are many ways to deploy software: it is now left up to you, your environment and budget to get things rolling.

How to get the ball rolling: Methods of deploying software.

Lets go from relatively simple and cost-free solutions to more expensive options.

Scripts.

We covered Batch scripts, mentioned Power Shell, and there are a lot of different "flavors" of scripting that have their ups and downs. Many prefer to script with Perl

Logon Scripts.

Logon Scripts can be used locally or via your Directory Service. These can contain Directory Service specific commands (eDirectory, for example, has a set of commands and variables that you can use, like Computername, Username, etc.), call executable files or other batch scripts each time the user logs on.

Group Policies.

If you are using an Active Directory environment (all your users and computers integrate with the directory service of a Microsoft server in your domain), you can give software deployment a thought, as this is possible with Group Policies.

What is a group policy?

Basically put, this is a set of rules you can define for all kinds of objects in your Active Directory, like users, computers, printers, etc.

Group Policies have the option of installing programs. When software is assigned to a user, it is installed when the user logs on into his or her computer. When assigned to a computer, it is installed when the computer starts, has contact with the Active Directory and receives the instructions to install.

you can assign software and publish software: assigning means that the software will be installed once the user or workstation receives its updated Group Policy; assigning means that the user will receive an icon, and the software installs itself when the icon is executed[37].

Please bear in mind:

Rolling out software via GPO is not a substitute for "complete" software deployment.

What you cannot control via GPO is:

- Timing. Software installations happen when users log in or their client machines boot. Urgent deployments or scheduled installations are not possible.

- Reporting. GPO pushes the installation, but does not necessarily do any manageable reporting (Did the installation fail? Where was it successful? When? This all would have to be done via manually writing some kind of log file with a script within the installation. In short: possible, but painful.)

---

[37] http://support.microsoft.com/kb/816102/en-us

- Security. Installation requires elevated privileges on the client. If all your clients have elevated privileges, (which might raise an eyebrow here or there from security administrators), then it should be no problem. If not, then you will need workarounds for some software packages; as they will install as the logged on user and use his or her rights. Tools like "runas" or "setacl[38]" could be of help, but then you will have problems with exposed passwords).

To completely manage your software deployments (distributing, logging, dependencies, advanced grouping, security and the like), you would need a professional software distribution suite: we will have a look at one of these in the following chapters. We will have a look at ZenWorks Configuration Management; we have had great experiences with this powerful set of tools. This book does not want to especially endorse the use of this software, it just wants to show you how these software utilities "tick" and what is possible.

Software Distributions Suites.

There are many, many software suites out there that cover the basic endpoint / client management and much, much more. Core services are:

- Mobile Device Management
- IT Asset Management
- IT Service Management
- Client Management
- Operating System Rollout

---

[38] http://technet.microsoft.com/en-us/library/dd315261

We are going to have a peek at ZENworks Configuration Management[39], and here are some honorable mentions:

- **Matrix42**
    - o http://www.matrix42.com/

- **Altiris**
    - o http://www.symantec.com/configuration-management

- **Baramundi**
    - o http://www.baramundi.com/

- **Dell Kace**
    - o http://www.kace.com/

- **Microsoft System Center Configuration Manager**
    - O http://www.microsoft.com/en-us/server-cloud/system-center/configuration-manager-2012.aspx

Read on to the next chapter to find out more about a great example of a Software Management Suite: ***ZenWorks Configuration Management.***

---

[39] http://www.novell.com/products/zenworks/configurationmanagement/

Dennis B. Waldon

Chapter 16: ZenWorks Configuration Management

Lets have a peek at the ZenWorks Configuration Suite from Novell.

Definition

What is ZenWorks? According to the Wiki Website[40], "ZCM is a full solution for the full lifecycle management of a Windows workstation, from initial imaging to deploying applications (bundles), policies (Group Policies, Dynamic Local User etc.), asset inventory and management/reconciliation of licensing and more.

ZCM supports Windows and Linux server platforms, and all currently supported Windows desktop environments (XP, Vista and Windows 7)."

ZCM has a Web Administration Interface, giving a quick overview of all Servers, Workstations, Policies and Bundles and their status. Clicking on any kind of object takes you right to a more detailed overview. The following screenshot shows a very basic overview of the servers, workstations, policies and bundles in ZCM.

This tool is powerful: it has many features specifically made for installing, patching, maintaining , reporting your environment, licensing and managing your assets, all in one interface.

Message Summary	⊗	◇	◉	Total
Servers	4	0	2	6
Workstations	8	0	25	33
Policies	0	0	37	37
Bundles	8	0	1377	1385

Picture 65 - A brief overview of messages in ZCM

40

http://wiki.novell.com/index.php/ZENworks/ZCM:ZENworks_Configuration_Management_10# What_Is_ZCM.3F

That about wraps up everything you would need to manage your Windows environment.

Terminologies

ZCM uses terms and phrases that one should know about; getting to know these makes working with this suite a whole lot easier.

Relationships.

As in real life, ZenWorks is all about *relationships*. *Users*, *groups* of users, *machines*, *groups* of machines, *software bundles* (explained later) and *software bundle groups* and *policies* all have some kind of relationship to one another.

A user can be "related" to one single machine, a group of machines, one or more policies, all based on a relationship. This can also be seen the other way round: machines can be "related" to a user or a group of users or a whole set of policies, depending on how these relationships are set.

The following screenshot shows a Software Bundle and the way it can be related to other objects. you can assign 7Zip (our favorite choice of open source file compressor / decompressor), to a device, group of devices, users or groups of users. The great thing is, distributing is made really simple.

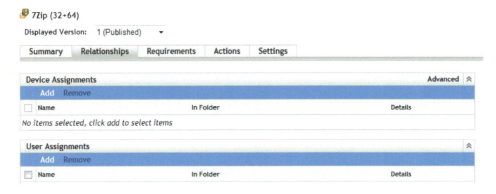

Picture 66 - Relationships are defined here in the "Relationships" Tab

Groups (and Dynamic Groups)

you most probably will not manage each and every one of your users and machines and software bundles *individually*. These objects can be grouped together, either manually or dynamically, and then have settings, bundles and policies applied to them.

Dynamic groups are groups of objects that automatically come together based on a certain criteria.

If you set a dynamic group of machines with the settings of its members having to have Windows 7 64 bit and, lets say, at least 4 GB of RAM, all machines in your hard- and software environment meeting that criteria will be associated with that group. It is "dynamic" in that all new or changed objects that meet the criteria of the dynamic group are automatically added. If a machine is upgraded with RAM, it meets the requirements of that group and is added.

Users

Users are pretty much, next to the software packages, the core elements of ZCM.

They can be imported and kept in sync from a variety of sources like eDirectory & Active Directory.

This makes your job a whole lot easier: you can manage your users, machines and groups of such in one place.

Software Bundles

Software bundles are "packages": they include all that is necessary for software installations (files, actions to be taken with these files, dependencies, etc.).

These can be MSI files, setups with their additional files, etc. Whole directories can also be uploaded and then downloaded on the client for execution of setups.

The following screenshot shows an example of various software bundles shown in ZCM.

Bundles > Systemsoftware

Bundles

📁 New ▾ Edit ▾ Delete Action ▾ Quick Tasks ▾

	Status	Name ▲	Type	Category	Enabled	Versio
☐		📁 7Zip (Details)	Folder			
☐		📁 Adobe Flash Player (Details)	Folder			
☐		📁 BGinfo (Details)	Folder			
☐		📁 CD Burner XP (Details)	Folder			

Picture 67 - A list of Software Bundles in ZCM

Software bundles can be scheduled to install at a certain time or at certain events (User Logons or Logoffs, machine boots, etc.). They can also just be made available via link, and automatically install when the user first wants to use them.

Software Bundle Groups

It is a really practical function to group Software Bundles. Say you have systems that need a certain piece of software that will always need *other* certain software to run.

Example: a "Standard" Client may need an office program, a PDF reader and certain plugins for browsers.

you might, in this case, bundle each of these pieces of software individually, and then group them together, and then distribute this bundle group. you can always change one of these programs without having to re-distribute all the rest. Why is this so important?

Never, *never* create one huge software bundle with several software packages all glued / mixed in one: if you change one single setting, your whole bundle has to be redistributed. This takes tons of time depending on your bundle, and takes unnecessary resources in your network when deploying again.

Always keep this simple rule in mind:

Create *single* packages, and then *group* or *chain* them together (if they logically belong to each other).

you can create a chain (better known as a dependency) of applications: this basically means that if product C is to be installed, ZCM has to install product N first and *then* continue with installation).

Machine Groups

The following screenshot shows an example of dynamic machine groups: each machine group contains machines that meet a certain criteria: in this case different operating systems. In this case, a machine can "logically" only belong to one group, unless that machine has different operating systems installed on the hard disk and they are booted separately and reporting to the ZCM Server.

Picture 68 - Brief overview of Devices in the GUI

Red Hat Enterprise Linux Desktop 4	Dynamic Workstation Group
Red Hat Enterprise Linux Desktop 5	Dynamic Workstation Group
Red Hat Enterprise Linux Desktop 6	Dynamic Workstation Group
SUSE Linux Enterprise Desktop 10	Dynamic Workstation Group
SUSE Linux Enterprise Desktop 11	Dynamic Workstation Group
Windows 2000 Workstations	Dynamic Workstation Group
Windows 7 Workstations	Dynamic Workstation Group
Windows Vista Workstations	Dynamic Workstation Group
Windows XP Workstations	Dynamic Workstation Group

Picture 69 - A list of Dynamic Groups based on Operating Systems

Policies[41]

Policies can apply to different aspects: you have User policies, Printer Policies, Bookmark Policies, Remote Management Policy, Windows Group Policy, and more.

---

[41]

http://www.novell.com/documentation/zenworks11/zen11_cm_policies/?page=/documentation/zenworks11/zen11_cm_policies/data/bb2h0as.html

☐		DLU-Notebooks-Administrator	Dynamic Local User Policy	Yes
☐		DLU-Notebooks-User	Dynamic Local User Policy	Yes
☐		PRN-Notebook-Win7-64Bit	Printer Policy	Yes
☐		REM-User Notebooks	Remote Management Policy	Yes
☐		REM-Workstation Notebooks	Remote Management Policy	Yes

Picture 70 - A list of Policies in ZCM

These policies define what a user, printer, Windows Group Policy, etc. should look like and behave.

Each of these policies are a set of rules that you give an object (like a user, computer, or group of).

Lets say you have a certain group of computers or users in a department. you can create a printer policy (printer driver and its settings) that will apply for all computers or only certain users in a certain IP range.

The Client
All clients have a so-called *agent* installed. This agent keeps communication open with the ZCM server, and listens for commands. It is responsible for reporting the status of its machine and the software installed or to be installed.

This agent also completes the actions given from the ZCM server, actions like install, uninstall, copy jobs and the like.

Once software is bundled and assigned, a link can be created on the Desktop, Start Menu or *Application Explorer* (a special folder created by ZCM on the client). you can tell a ZenWorks application by the little icon.

The first screenshot shows an installed application (notice the little "Z" on the bottom left corner of the icon):

Picture 71- An installed ZCM Software Bundle

Our second screenshot shows an application that is made available, but not installed yet (notice the little grey "X" on the top left).

Picture 72 - An application not installed but ready

A look at the Web administration: Software Bundles

The following sections will give you a look at the Software Deployment features of ZCM.

As you can see in the following screenshot, you can create as many "folders" (logical folders where you can keep different software packages sorted) as you need in the ZenWorks interface.

This helps you organize your software bundles.

Bundles > Systemsoftware

Picture 73 - Software Bundles in the ZCM Gui

Bundle Details

The web administration gives you many options and information on the status of your bundles.

In the following screenshot, you can see information like:

- Bundle Type

- Version (each time you tweak of change your Software Bundle, the version can be raised and ZenWorks automatically re-issues the Software Bundle)

- Relationships (mentioned before)

- Requirements (like: how much RAM does the machine have to have, what Operating System version,....)

- Bundle Activity (shows the User what it is doing: like showing a progress bar when installing)

A Beginners Guide to Software Deployment

Bundles > Systemsoftware > 7Zip > 7Zip (32+64)

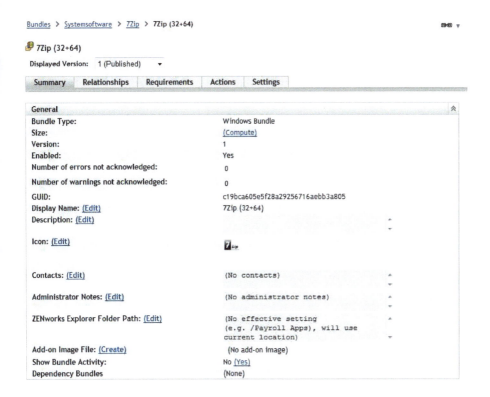

7Zip (32+64)

Displayed Version: 1 (Published) ▼

| Summary | Relationships | Requirements | Actions | Settings |

General ⌃

Bundle Type:	Windows Bundle
Size:	(Compute)
Version:	1
Enabled:	Yes
Number of errors not acknowledged:	0
Number of warnings not acknowledged:	0
GUID:	c19bca605e5f28a29256716aebb3a805
Display Name: (Edit)	7Zip (32+64)
Description: (Edit)	
Icon: (Edit)	
Contacts: (Edit)	(No contacts)
Administrator Notes: (Edit)	(No administrator notes)
ZENworks Explorer Folder Path: (Edit)	(No effective setting (e.g. /Payroll Apps), will use current location)
Add-on Image File: (Create)	(No add-on image)
Show Bundle Activity:	No (Yes)
Dependency Bundles	(None)

Picture 74 - An overview of a Software Bundle in ZCM

Bundle Actions

This is where it gets interesting: the "heart" of your application. Once you have created a folder, you can create a software bundle. As mentioned, this can be an MSI, a single setup file, even a whole directory that is copied and downloaded on the client and then executed. This can also be a script / batch file or a simple copy job.

you can tell ZenWorks *what*, *how* and *when* it should be doing something. These can all be created in steps that follow one after the other. What we want to focus on in the following screenshot are the:

- Install
- Launch
- Verify and
- Uninstall

features.

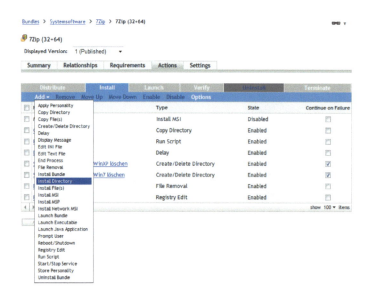

Picture 75 - The Install, Launch, Verify and Uninstall options

Install Section

As you can see, "Install" offers many options. We want to discuss the most common of all:

Copy files / Directories

Sometimes a program is a single file or a directory that can be copied from another source without the need of a "real" setup or installation. Maybe you want to place a whole directory on your local machine, and then run the setup from there. This option would be the right place to go for this action. you can also upload a directory to the ZCM Server with "Install Directory", and this will then be copied to the client machine.

Remove files

This option is practical as it can be used to either "clean up" after an installation, or make sure that something is removed before your Bundle starts to get installed.

Install Bundle

you can "chain" installations this way, or make sure that other programs are also installed that need to go along with your bundle. Imagine you have an in house application that needs to be installed. That application may need a PDF Reader, and a special kind of viewer.

Bundling everything into one big bundle is a bad idea. Why? Well, if you need to make a change (newer PDF Reader, different Viewer), you will have to change the WHOLE bundle.

If you split your bundles, you can install the viewer on some workstations, the PDF on all workstations, and if you install the in house application, "chain" the other two with your in house application so that they are installed along with your application. Any changes to the Viewer or Reader are independent of your bundle group.

Delay

Pretty much self-explanatory: sometimes there is no other way than to build in a timed delay before the next step in the installation should start.

Install an MSI or MSP

you can upload Windows Installer files and ZCM uses those features of Windows Installer to install MSIs or patches.

Launch Executable

This lets you launch an executable, with option parameters (this could be a setup.exe or whatever program you want started). Due to the fact that most users have no administrator privileges, this can be executed with help of the ZCM agent and its rights.

Edit Registry

you can either create your own registry values in the editor or upload a registry file with values and then distribute them.

Run Script

This part runs a script on your client machine. This can be a script that is already installed on your machine (with or without the help of ZCM), or can be edited directly in ZCM and then executed on the client.

Uninstall Bundle

Simply said: this performs the steps specified in the uninstallation of a Bundle (more in a few pages).

Start / Stop Services

This tool can start and stop services (often necessary during installations / uninstallations).

Launch Section

The Launch tab of a software bundle tells the ZCM agent what to launch, or start when the software bundle is to begin. The software bundle –first- looks to see if any Install actions are to be completed, and then it launches. A launch could be a simple call to a command (Notepad.exe), or it could be chained like our previous example in the Install section. Maybe you want certain files to be overwritten before the program starts, then you want an executable to be called. It is all possible with ZCM.

Verify

Verify is pretty much a "fix" for an installation. Lets say the configuration of a program or the program installation is corrupted on a client. you can enable the verify option, and the client can repeat the steps of the installation to "fix" the software bundle. Really simple if it is MSI; then the Windows Installer tries to fix the bundle with MSI mechanisms. Otherwise, the steps give in the Install tab are repeated, and the "Launch" action is executed in the end.

Uninstall Section

This basically uninstalls a software bundle. If it is an MSI bundle, it will be relatively easy, as ZCM uses the Windows Installer with all its comfortable options.

As in the previous example, you can chain actions: maybe you want to stop a certain Windows service first, or place files on the machine for the uninstall. you can also remove certain files manually if you want to at the end of an installation.

If the software bundle was installed via a scripted installer, you will have to specify what executable to run with the needed parameters. Be aware of using silent uninstalls, otherwise your users may be confronted with an uninstall screen. (Can lead to uninstall cancellations or other problems).

It can be a bit challenging if the software bundle had a lot of "manual" steps involved in the installation. you would then create a reverse logic of an installation: stop a certain service or process, run an uninstaller, or simply remove files and settings and registry entries with the help of ZCM.

In a Nutshell

As mention before, this tool is a powerful one: it has many features specifically made for installing, patching, maintaining and reporting your environment, all in one interface.

Chapter 17: Uninstallation & Uninstallation Troubleshooting

Introduction

Uninstalling a program silently can be a challenge.

If the program was installed via Windows Installer, the uninstallation process is rather easy.

Using the options mentioned before with Windows Installer, and knowing the Product ID, you can very quickly uninstall a program.

Other installers, depending also on their version, use different ways to uninstall a program.

Sometimes a specific uninstall program is delivered, and sometimes a setup.exe, copied to a hidden location, coupled with the correct parameters will uninstall the application.

If you have a look at the Windows installed programs applet in the Control Panel, you will see the list of installed programs on your computer. How does Windows know what to do when told to uninstall a program?

Avira Free Antivirus	Avira	09.05.2012	139 MB
Microsoft .NET Framework 4 Client Profile	Microsoft Corporation	27.10.2011	120 MB
Blender	Blender Foundation	14.07.2012	115 MB
Origin	Electronic Arts, Inc.	09.06.2012	110 MB
K-Lite Codec Pack 7.6.0 (Full)		27.08.2011	49,8 MB
Microsoft .NET Framework 3.5 SP1	Microsoft Corporation	30.06.2012	37,2 MB
Microsoft .NET Framework 3.5 Language Pack SP1 - DEU	Microsoft Corporation	30.08.2011	36,9 MB
Mozilla Firefox 7.0.1 (x86 de)	Mozilla	06.12.2011	32,8 MB
GPL Ghostscript	Artifex Software Inc.	22.09.2011	31,5 MB
Adobe AIR	Adobe Systems Incorporated	27.08.2011	30,1 MB

Picture 76 - The Application Wizard

Dennis B. Waldon

Welcome to the Windows Registry.

Here is where the uninstall actions are stored.

The best place to go to would be the following branch:

[HKEY_LOCAL_MACHINE\SOFTWARE\Microsoft\Windows\CurrentVersion\U ninstall\.

Here is what Windows is told what to do when uninstalling a program.

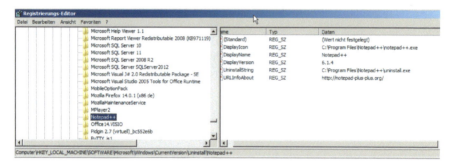

Here you will find a seemingly cryptic branch of product codes and names of programs.

Within each of these branches, you will find various settings, and one of these is the UninstallString.

MSI Installations

If it is a MSI installation, you will most probably find a

msiexec.exe /X {PRODUCTNUMBER} or a msiexec /I{PRODUCTNUMBER}.

These will guide you through the same process as installation, but with the option of either uninstalling changing the installation or changing it. Using the **/qn** or **/qb** switches will help you get your program uninstalled *silently*.

Other uninstallers

If it is not a MSI installation, you might have to do some research and digging to both cleanly and silently remove this program. We already showed you some parameters for different installers; if you know which installer was used, you can try out those uninstall parameters.

A program may simply list the *UninstallString* value as a "c:\program files\application\setup.exe /REMOVE. Which may leave you stumped as how to uninstall it without user interaction.

Tip 1: Find the setup.exe file given in the UninstallString value in the Registry on your hard drive. From the command prompt, type "setup.exe" (or the .exe that is given) with the "/?" option. Sometimes uninstall options, and even silent uninstall options are displayed.

Tip 2: Use the internet to find out either from the manufacturer's support site how to uninstall or silently uninstall the program, or search 3rd party websites that list experiences of how users found out how to uninstall this program. A great resource is ITNinja (www.itninja.com)

Tip 3: Try common commands. Trying options like "-silent", "-verysilent", "-quiet" can help!

Here is the quote we mentioned a few chapters ago:

"To make an educated guess about how to run an installer unattended, you need to know which system was used to create it. Sometimes this will be obvious from the installer's splash screen; sometimes you can figure it out by running strings; and sometimes you will have to guess."[42]

Tip 4: If all else fails, you might have to delete any services, executables and files manually.

---

[42] http://unattended.sourceforge.net/installers.php

The End – Where do we go from here?

That's it! This should definitely get you started on your path of software deployment. There are tons of further documentation on the web; this book is a brief compilation of the different directions you can go.

We hope you had as much fun reading as we did compiling and building this book! Feel free to experiment and if at first you don't succeed; try, try again!

We would appreciate your feedback!

Write anytime to dennis.waldon@gmail.com.

Follow me on Twitter! @dennisbwaldon

and Facebook: http://www.facebook.com/dennisbwaldon

- Dennis

www.ingramcontent.com/pod-product-compliance
Lightning Source LLC
Chambersburg PA
CBHW041142050326
40689CB00001B/447